The Greatest Networker in the World

John Milton Fogg

PRIMA PUBLISHING

PRIMA PUBLISHING and colophon are registered trademarks of Prima Communications, Inc.

Library of Congress cataloging-in-publication data on file
0-7615-1057-5

01 HH 10 9 8 7 6
Printed in the United States of America

How to Order
Single copies may be ordered from Prima Publishing, 3000 Lava Ridge Court, Roseville, CA 95661; telephone (800) 632-8676. Quantity discounts are also available. On your letterhead, include information concerning the intended use of the books and the number of books you wish to purchase.

Visit us online at www.primalifestyles.com

Dedication

To partnership and the two most
empowering partners in the world—

Susan Fogg and John Mann

. . . *We entered the restaurant with the maître d' and the Greatest Networker appearing to be the very best of friends; and I noticed smiling exchanges passing constantly between my host and an assortment of waiters and customers. As we took our seats, I noted, "You certainly live in a different world than I do."*

"How's that?" he asked.

"Well, everybody is all smiles and warmth and friendship ... you seem to know everybody, and they all know you and like you. Do you own this place or something?"

Another booming laugh. I was becoming a little less self-conscious about that.

"Tell me," he asked, "what's present for you when all of this 'smiling and friendshipping,' as you call it, is going on?"

What a question. "'Present'?" I asked, "what do you mean?"

"What's here, like in the air around us—what do you notice is present for you?"

I took a deep breath—I was getting used to his unique kind of questions, too. So I answered thoughtfully. "I feel envious," I told him, "and curious, too. I want to know how I can have my life be like this."

"Tell me," he asked, leaning closer and looking very directly, yet not at all threateningly, into my face, "what do you really want your life to be like?" . . .

Contents

CHAPTER ONE
The End

I 'll never forget that evening. That was the night I first met the Greatest Networker in the World. It was also (as I've heard a number of very successful Network Marketers say since) the night my life changed for the better—forever!

First, I suppose I should tell you what my life was like at that point.

I'd been involved with this one particular Network Marketing company for a little over four months and it wasn't going very well. In fact, it was looking a lot like a bad joke.

The products were great—everybody I shared them with agreed with that. But for the life of me, I couldn't get anyone interested in my business opportunity. I was working 30 hours a week *part-time*—all my evenings and most of my weekends— and what I had to show for it was a retail profit of $150 to $200 a month!

Like I said, "Ha ha."

I'd figured it out once: my home-based "wave of the future" business was earning me a handsome $1.56 an hour—*gross!* My kids were strangers. My wife was disenchanted and so distant she might as well have lived in Alaska! Clearly, this Networking business was not for me, nor was I for it.

I'd made up my mind. This was my last opportunity meeting.

The hotel room was packed, as usual. When I walked in, I noticed a particularly large swarm of people gathered around someone in the front of the room. I took aside a distributor I'd met before, pointed to the group and asked, "Who's that over there with all those people around him?"

"Oh," she said, "that's the Greatest Networker in the World . . . would you like to meet him?"

"Sure," I said. She took me over.

The man in the middle was strikingly handsome—well-groomed, looked to be in his early forties, elegantly dressed, yet not at all showy. He was clearly successful and wore it well.

His clothes were expensive: British suit with real button-holes, great floral tie and a breast pocket scarf quietly but noticeably picking up the burgundy reds of the tie . . . and, yes, there was the gold Rolex Oyster I expected, peeking out from beneath his cuff-linked shirt.

I noticed that his shirt was monogrammed on the cuff, but the stitches of the initials were the exact same color thread as the shirt. Subtle, classy touch, I told myself.

Just then there was a brief opening in the crowd around

the man and my friend pulled me into the "inner circle."
The Greatest Networker was listening intently to what a
woman standing directly in front of me was saying, when his
eye caught mine. He put a hand on the woman's shoulder and
asked her to excuse him for just a moment. Then he looked
me straight in the face, extended his hand to me, and said,
with a warmth that actually shocked me with its intensity:
"Hello. It's really good to see you." He told me his name
and asked me mine.

Now, normally I'm able to say who I am with ease. Not this
time. I stammered—actually, I *stuttered*, something I hadn't
done in 25 years. His grip on my hand became a bit firmer and
he asked, "How are you doing?"

I said something conventional—I can't remember exactly
what. Something like, "Fine, thanks." And he replied, "*Really*, is that true?"

Before I had time to stop myself with a polite avoidance of
his question, I found myself telling him how I was *really* doing. He listened to me in a way I've never experienced before.
I actually *felt* him listening to me. It was, well, *physical*.

Amazing!

I told him how my business—and my life—were going.
There it was, all out in the open and on the table. And I told
him this was my last opportunity meeting, that I wasn't cut
out for Network Marketing. I think I told him, "It just isn't
my thing." He smiled. I suddenly realized that throughout our
brief conversation, he still had hold of my hand. He squeezed
it again, just then, and asked, "Would you have some time
after the meeting to spend with me?"

Before I could get my defensive "No" plus an excuse out of

my mouth, I heard myself say, "Gosh, that would be great."

"Gosh . . . "—I sounded like a teenager.

He smiled again. Thanked me. Said he'd see me after the meeting, turned back to the woman with whom he'd been speaking and walked and talked with her, taking a seat in the front section close to the right of the stage.

I sat in the far back of the room in what had become "my" seat. It was, I'd come to learn, a seat in my "comfort zone." It was a place to hide, and I knew that.

After the formal part of the meeting was over and the groups of new distributors and their sponsors were leaving together, he came up to me where I was standing by the coat rack. He smiled at me with that same noticeable warmth as before, and I pointed to his smiling face and said, "You know, if I could find a way to package that smile of yours, I'd have the perfect product. I'd be rich in a couple of weeks!"

His laughter came so quickly and boomed so loudly all around the room, everybody who was left turned to look at us. I was very self-conscious.

"That's great!" he exclaimed. "Thanks! It is a good smile, isn't it? Well, I'll tell you, I built this smile myself—tooth by tooth. My smile wasn't always like this.

"Yes," he continued, "I am proud of this smile," and he flashed the grin even bigger than before. "It *feels* wonderful, too!

"Come on," he said, taking me by the arm and moving off through the door. "Let's get some coffee and something to eat. Have you had dinner?"

I said I'd grabbed a quick bag of nuts before the meeting.

"Trail mix?" he asked.

"Something like that," I said. "Got it from the gift shop downstairs."

"I've had dinner there myself," he said. "The food and service aren't very good. The selection is limited. It's pretty pricy, too. You know," he laughed, "that gift shop is a truly disappointing restaurant!"

I agreed—laughing right along with him. It felt good to be with him. He'd certainly changed the way I was feeling in a remarkably short time.

"So, what do you like to eat most?" he asked.

And before I could say something polite—and not the truth—he added, "It's a sincere question. What would you *most* like to eat—right now?"

I took a deep breath and said, "Italian."

"Great!" he said. "Me too. Can I take you to a place I just love? It's only ten minutes away."

"Your car or mine?" I asked.

"Let's take mine," he said. "It's right out front."

* * *

I don't know what I expected the Greatest Networker in the World to drive. Something exotic . . . certainly *very* expensive, so I was quite shocked when the doorman greeted us and walked us over to open the passenger-side door of what I guessed to be a mid-'70s Ford pickup truck. Painted simply in gray primer, no less!

I guess he saw the disappointment or whatever the look

was on my face. He laughed and asked, "You look like you were expecting something else?"

"Yes, I was."

"What did you expect?"

"I don't know—a Mercedes . . . a Porsche . . . maybe a Rolls Royce or something."

His laughter boomed around the enclosed hotel entrance. This guy seemed to laugh from his toes, not his mouth. The doorman was smiling, as well.

"Yes," he said, "I have those, but I like my truck best. You know, Sam Walton is the richest man in America, worth about $22 billion all told—and he drives a pickup. If it's good enough for Uncle Sam . . . ." And he let the rest of the sentence hang in the air.

He handed the doorman a $10 bill. Thanked him and said he hoped to see him soon. Then he stopped, as if remembering something, and asked the young man, "How's your business, Chris?"

The young doorman—a college-kid type—replied, "It's just great, sir. I made Supervisor last month. And thanks for introducing me to Barbara. She's the greatest!"

"Good," said the Greatest Networker. "You work hard, Chris, and you're smart. You deserve your success. What's up next for you?"

"Well," the young man answered thoughtfully, "I'll stay here at the hotel for another month or three. You were right about this place," the young man said looking up at the hotel. "I've met some of my best people here. I've got some traveling I want to do. I've got a great group going in San Antonio and I think I'll go down there for a few months. After that—who knows? Germany . . . Japan, maybe?"

"Let me know your plans. I know some people in Japan you might enjoy meeting," said my new friend.

"Thanks, I will," replied the young man earnestly, and I could tell by his tone that he would indeed do that.

"Have a great evening, Chris," the Greatest Networker called out as we drove off.

* * *

As we traveled to the restaurant, we made small talk. Actually, I made small talk. He just kept asking me questions.

He asked me where I lived . . . what part of town . . . how I liked it . . . what my neighbors were like . . . what my house was like . . . how my kids liked it and what their schools were like. I don't mean to make it sound like an interrogation. It wasn't that at all. He just seemed so curious, so interested in me—and so easy to talk to. I probably told him more about my life in those ten short minutes than I'd ever told anyone before.

When we got to the restaurant, a uniformed man came out and greeted us warmly, opened my door and asked me, was this my first time at his restaurant?

I told him it was, and he said how it was nice to see me and how he hoped I'd enjoy my dinner, and he suggested that if I truly liked great fresh fish, there was an absolutely terrific snapper cacciatore on the menu that he highly recommended.

I thanked him, feeling a little clumsy. I wasn't used to such treatment from anyone, let alone from the doorman at what looked to be a first-class establishment.

We entered the restaurant with the maître d' and the Greatest Networker appearing to be the very best of friends; and I noticed smiling exchanges passing constantly between my host and an assortment of waiters and customers. As we took our seats, I noted, "You certainly live in a different world than I do."

"How's that?" he asked.

"Well, everybody is all smiles and warmth and friendship . . . you seem to know everybody, and they all know you and like you. Do you own this place or something?"

Another booming laugh. I was becoming a little less self-conscious about *that*.

"Tell me," he asked, "what's present for you when all of this 'smiling and friendshipping,' as you call it, is going on?"

What a question. " 'Present'?" I asked, "what do you mean?"

"What's here, like in the air around us—what do you notice is present for you?"

I took a deep breath—I was getting used to his unique kind of questions, too. So I answered thoughtfully. "I feel envious," I told him, "and curious, too. I want to know how I can have my life be like this."

"Tell me," he asked, leaning closer and looking very directly, yet not at all threateningly, into my face, "what do you really want your life to be like?"

And so began a two-hour-plus dinner—the best I've ever eaten *and* spoken. All he did was ask me questions, followed by, " . . . Tell me more about that . . . " or, " . . . Can you say more about that?" And all I did was to tell him things I hadn't ever shared with anyone, not even with my wife!

[8]

A number of times during our dinner conversation, he asked questions to make sure he understood what I was saying. But there was something odd about them to me, because he'd ask me if such and such were true, even though I'd never actually *said* that particular "such and such."

I know, that's not very clear—is it? Let me give you an example.

I was talking about a job I'd had early on with a computer company back in Cambridge, Massachusetts. Calling it a "company" was a bit of a stretch. It was really just a bunch of guys—"hackers," we were called—who were messing around in the early days of computers. It was an exciting time for me. The work was fun, the people were wild—very smart and very stimulating. I'd had a good time back then.

He asked me, "So, you're a pioneer?"

See what I mean?

"*Pioneer?*" I said back to him. "No, I'm no pioneer. I was just having fun—it was in the early days of computers and we just played with stuff, that's all."

"Had anyone ever done that before?" he asked me.

I guessed not, I thought, and told him so.

And again he said, "So, you're a pioneer?"

I must have looked at him strangely, for he leaned back on his chair and gave a medium version of his booming laugh. I was no longer embarrassed by these mini-volcanos of mirth—and the folks in the restaurant, which had thinned out considerably by now, seemed more comfortable with them, too. They just turned to him and smiled, and then went back to their conversations.

"Ah . . . man," I stammered, "you've sure got a way of disarming me. Well, I suppose I *was* a pioneer . . . in a way . . . back then."

He looked surprised, and asked, " . . . back then?—Not now?"

Was he unreasonable or what? "Okay," I said—and I let my irritation show a little, "I'm a pioneer. But I seem to have lost my covered wagon . . ." And the moment I said it, I could literally feel what he was going to say next. Something about a "vehicle." I was certain of it.

But he didn't say a thing.

Silence.

I was very uncomfortable.

At last, he asked, "What were you thinking just now?"

"When?" I asked him back—a little *too* quickly. Then I held up my hand and shook my head saying, "No, wait. I know when. It's just . . . well, I . . . Oh, I don't know.

"Look, where's all of this going?" I asked him. "I mean, you're asking me questions and saying things to me that nobody's ever said to me before. Things that stop me cold and I don't know what to say to you . . . or even what to think."

He didn't say a word—just leaned forward, ever so slightly, and turned his head to the right and toward me just a bit, as if he wanted to make sure to catch every syllable I uttered. It was an intriguing expression—expectant, as if he were waiting to hear what I'd say next, and empathetic, as if he'd already completely accepted what I said, even though he didn't know what it was yet. It was comforting—and disarming at the same time.

I felt the air go out of me—and feelings well up inside me. Big feelings. Important ones. I felt suddenly very sad.

"I just want to be a success," I told him, emotion troubling my words a little. "I'm so sick and tired of the sameness . . . of not having the money to do what I want . . . to give my wife and kids the things they deserve. Disney World," I said, "I want to take the kids to Disney World—and the Grand Canyon. I want to be free. I want time . . . creativity . . . control . . . And yes, I do want to be a pioneer—again. I loved doing that . . . ."

"But . . . ?" he asked quietly.

"But, *I don't know how*," I answered, and I was certain I sounded close to crying. "I've heard all that positive mental attitude stuff, a hundred times—a thousand times. It doesn't work for me. Network Marketing doesn't work for me. Or, I guess, I don't work for it. Something like that.

"I see other people doing it. Lots of them. So I know it can be done. And I know they're not any smarter or better than me, or work any harder. It's just that—I can't seem to get it to work for me. I try. I really do. I make the calls . . . run my names list. It just doesn't work."

I looked over at him and asked, "What's wrong with me?"

He let his head fall back and looked up at the ceiling. He scrunched his shoulders up and down, took a big, long, deep breath and leveled his eyes on me.

"Look, how would you like me to show you how to do this business?"

"Are you kidding?" I asked, in a voice that had everybody in the restaurant turn and look over at us. "You bet!" I exclaimed, holding my excitement down to the dullest possible roar.

"Good," he said, matter-of-factly. "We'll start tomorrow. Here's what I want you to do . . . ."

He handed me a piece of paper on which he had written an address. He told me that was where he lived and to come to his office the next afternoon after I got off work. It looked to be about 90 minutes out of town, so said I could be there by 6:30, and he said that was perfect.

He reached into his briefcase and took out a package, wrapped in a glossy forest green paper. From its size and shape, I guessed it was a book.

"Here," he said, "this is your homework. I want you to read this before we meet tomorrow—okay?"

"The whole thing?" I asked.

"Yes," he said, pretending to be stern, but then he smiled and added, "Don't worry. It's a *very* quick read."

He paid for dinner. I thanked him. He thanked *everybody* in the restaurant.

He drove me back to the hotel where the meeting had been and where my car was parked. This time, I turned the tables on him and asked all about where he lived, his house, his neighbors . . . After four or five of my questions, he turned to me and smiled. "Bright boy. You learn quickly," he said.

That felt pretty good.

He left me next to my car, said goodbye and drove off in his truck.

I watched him go—watched him long after he'd gone from my sight. Then I unlocked my car, got in, turned the key, and sat there letting it warm up, staring blankly in front of me.

The book! I thought, and hurriedly pulled it out from my jacket pocket. I tore off the slick paper wrapping and turned it right-side up to read the title. Even in the dim light of the street lamp, the bold gold foil letters jumped off the deep green, glossy cover. They said:

What You Don't Know
That You Don't Know

I opened the book with tremendous excitement, flipping quickly past the beginning pages. After 10 or 12 pages, I stopped cold. There was not a word in it.

Every page in the book was totally blank!

CHAPTER TWO

To Speak the Truth

Time literally crawled by on its hand and knees that next day. Besides, it was Friday—and Fridays were like that anyway.

At 3:30, I simply couldn't take it any more and left the office. I pulled out the address he had given me in the restaurant, grabbed my map to be sure of my directions, and headed north out of town.

I would be a full hour early—even if I did get lost. Heck with it, I thought, I'll read or listen to tapes. Then I laughed, thinking of the book he gave me. That's it, I'll read that, I said to myself, and laughed aloud.

In about 10 minutes, I was out of town and into the suburbs. Another 20 minutes, and I was driving through the rolling green and earth-brown hills of farm country that spread out like a checkered picnic blanket all the way up to the mountains north of the city.

What a day . . . a "Chamber of Commerce day," the kind

they picture on postcards. A motorcycle day, I thought, bringing back memories.

The sun was bright. The clouds were big and fluffy and I made animals out of their shapes as I drove along. I started singing—then abruptly turned on the radio—and then noticed what I'd just done. "How can I feel self-conscious while driving alone in my own car?" I thought silently. "What a funny man I am."

I had a pretty good idea of what his house would look like from our conversation on the way back from the restaurant. He told me I'd see it up on the hill beyond the pond through the trees as soon as I turned onto Huckleberry Lane and saw the long, gray, four-board wooden fence on my right.

Sure enough, there was the fence. I pulled over off the road, stopped my car, and leaned forward over the steering wheel to get a good look at the house and the property.

I don't know what architectural style it was. Not Tudor—that's the one with all that criss-crossed wood—but it was some kind of English looking. Big, but not overly imposing, although it certainly was, well . . . *more* than any house I'd ever visited before. It looked like something you'd see in a Jag or Rolls Royce ad in *Architectural Digest*.

This was a card-carrying *estate!*

There were a number of buildings around the main house. One was clearly a horse barn with a number of double-Dutch doors across the face of it. One looked like a small version of the big house—a guest house or carriage house, or something. There were a couple of others as well. All the buildings were painted the same light gray as the fence, with the woodwork a darker, charcoal gray, and all were covered with ivy. Everything was surrounded by trees —huge oaks, maples and pines. They were tall enough to have been there forever. Lots of shrubbery and flower gardens, too. It was simply magnificent! In fact, this was the kind of home I'd always dreamed of having.

From the road, the grounds all looked quite manicured, although there were woods to my right and they had a fair amount of underbrush mixed in among the trees.

And horses . . . there were six—no, *eight* of them grazing in the fields between the house and the road, maybe more. Beautiful horses, thoroughbreds by the look of them, and three were grays. I love horses—especially dapple gray ones. It had been a dream of mine to have horses, too. I got out to take a closer look.

As I got up to the paddock fence, I called out to the nearest of the horses. It lifted its head, saw me and immediately started trotting in my direction.

Just then, I noticed a horse and rider coming out of the near woods, cantering towards me. It was him.

The gray mare I'd called to and the Greatest Networker reached me at the same time.

"Well, you certainly got her attention. She doesn't come to just anybody. Rebecca's the only one she pays attention to," he said, swinging his leg over his mount's neck and sliding off the saddle in one easy, flowing movement. He's done that before, I thought.

"It's good to see you. You're an hour early," he noted without looking at his watch. "How are you?" He walked over to me and extended his hand between the top rails of the fence.

"I'm good," I replied, " . . . and a little nervous."

He laughed, another one of those booming laughs of his, and said, "You do learn quickly. Thanks for being so honest. What are you nervous about?"

"Well," I said as I pointed in a sweeping gesture that took in his property, "this isn't where I usually find myself on a Friday afternoon. This is . . . well . . . this is a pretty awesome place you've got."

"Yes, it is," he replied, joining me in looking appreciatively over the house, woods and fields.

"You know," I told him, "I have a dream of owning a place very much like this: horses, house, trees, and fields."

"Good," he said, "would you like to buy it?"

"*What?!*" I exclaimed.

"I'll sell it to you," he said, turning and looking me straight in the eyes in that provoking, gently confronting way of his.

"I doubt it's within my budget at the moment," I said, sarcastically.

"I don't remember saying how much I'd sell it for—did I?"

"No," I admitted, "you didn't."

"So how do you know whether or not it's within your budget?" he asked.

"Okay," I sighed. "How much?"

"Two point six million," he stated flatly. "Do you want to buy it?"

"*Stop it!*" I insisted—becoming irritated and letting it show. "This is ridiculous. You know I don't have that kind of money!"

"I don't know that," he said, looking calmly at me. "And that's not what I asked. I asked if you wanted to buy it. Do you—yes or no?"

"This is pointless," I snapped. "I can't even *conceive* of that much money. How . . ." He held up his hand—I stopped talking. I could feel the color flushing my cheeks. My legs had even started shaking. It was like I was about to get into a fight or something, and I was afraid.

"Yes or no?" he asked again. "Do you want to buy my house?"

"No. Don't be absurd," I said.

"I am not being absurd," he said. "However—you are! One of the most absurd things a person can do is to not tell the truth."

"W-what?" I stammered, amazed.

"You are lying," he said sternly. His eyes looked both mischievous and dead serious at the same time. I was stunned.

"Please," he prodded gently, "tell me if what I am about to say is true or not: You would love nothing more in this world than to buy my house. It would be a dream come true for you. I am not asking if you have the money. I am asking simply if you would like to buy my house—yes, or no?"

"Well, if you put it that way—yes, I'd love to buy your house."

He sighed, took a deep breath and smiled. "I do put it that way," he quoted me back to myself. "Tell me, do you often have difficulty answering the questions people ask you?"

"Well . . . " I started, but then shook my head and fell silent. I looked up at him, trying to read something from his face—hoping to find the right answer there somewhere.

"There is no right answer," he said, as if reading my mind. "There is only your answer, right now, to the question."

We stood in silence for some time. He—looking at me. Me—looking anywhere else but at him. When my eyes finally got up the courage to settle on his, he said, "Look, in our relationship together, I insist that you and I speak the truth. I think that will be difficult for you, because you don't listen, not yet. What you hear me saying is colored by what you say to yourself about what I am saying. Is that true?"

"Yes, it is," I told him.

He nodded and went on. "Did you read the book I gave you last night?"

I didn't know what to say to him. How do you read a book without a word in it?

"Yes or no?" he asked, patiently.

"Yes," I said.

"Well, what did you think?"

"I don't know . . . "

"*Good!*" he exclaimed. "Come on up to the house and tell me all about it."

I turned and numbly fumbled back to my car. I wasn't sure what to think. And so, for the moment, I tried to think nothing, and just watch where I was going.

CHAPTER THREE
The Secret Revealed

The house and it's surroundings were even more impressive from a closer look. Everything was just magnificent.

There was just the right amount of imperfection: white-wash (or rather, gray-wash) fading on the stones of the house, and a casual quality to the gardens that was all the more striking because of their lack of formality. The place wasn't stilted or uptight, as in some pictures I've seen of wealthy homes. People actually *lived* here—and as if to prove it, three bounding dogs happily greeted me as I got out of my car on the flagstone driveway.

"Ah, you've been properly greeted, I see," the Greatest Networker said, as he came through a doorway in a high stone wall that ran alongside the main house. "May I introduce you to Mr. and Mrs. Silver." He patted the heads of a huge, handsome pair of silver-gray standard poodles, their curly coats trimmed neatly in sporting cuts, without those poofy tufts of hair that make poodles look like topiary trees.

"And this is the Duchess," he said, ruffling the fur of a little black dog that clearly had lots of Border Collie in her. "Duchess has been with us only a couple of months," he told me, bending down to get an enthusiastic licking from a little mutt whose tail clearly was "wagging the dog."

"We think she'd been hit by a car," he said. "No one seems to know where she's from. She's adopted us for now.

"Come to my office." He stood up, and we walked over to the smaller house I'd seen from the road.

"I've worked from my home for years, but I think this is the best arrangement of all," he told me as we entered the building. "Having some physical separation between my 'home office' and home, yet having them this close to each other—it's perfect."

His office was comfortable and lived in, bright with sunlight, plants everywhere. Casual, comfortable elegance.

There were two parts to the first floor. Inside the entry was a living room with a small mahogany grand piano just in front of the windows; adjacent to the fireplace were two plump couches covered with what looked to be Native American blankets. These were facing each other across a coffee table with books "neatly scattered" on it and a clear, fish-bowl-like glass vase off to one side, out of which flowed a fountain of wildflowers—mostly daisies. There were Oriental carpets of varying sizes and colors on the wide-plank wooden floor, and a wide, sliding double-doorway—the kind where the doors disappear into the walls—that opened into a slightly smaller room off to the right with a huge, expansive desk thrust up like an island in the center of the room.

Both rooms were lined with paintings and over-filled book-shelves. I'd never seen so many books before.

"You've got quite a library," I observed. It was an under-statement in the extreme.

"Yes," he said, surveying what must have numbered well over a thousand volumes, perhaps more. "I love books. I love information of all kinds—do you?"

"Information?" That was a curious way to put it. "Sure," I said.

"So tell me," he asked, "what did you think about the book I gave you to read last night?"

"*What You Don't Know That You Don't Know?*" I asked.

"That's the one," he said, sitting down deep into one of the couches. "Of all the books I have ever read—that is the most important book of all."

I searched his face to make out his expression. I wondered if he were kidding . . . if he might be playing with me. He was looking straight at me—wide open, expressionless.

I sat down, too.

"Well . . . I don't know," I said.

"Good," he replied. "Perfect."

I wanted badly to have something profound to say—something that would show him . . . what? That would let him know I . . . but the truth was, I had nothing to tell him. I didn't know what to say.

"There's a story I want to tell you," he said, plainly coming to rescue me from my awkward silence. "Would you like to hear it?"

"Sure."

"In Japan, many years ago, it was the tradition among Buddhist monks to travel from monastery to monastery, seeking the teaching of the masters. As was the custom, the master would serve his guest tea and they would talk.

"One young monk was a particularly outstanding student. In fact, he was so exceptional, he had made a bit of a career out of showing up lesser masters with his skill and tremendous intelligence.

"One day, he called at a very famous monastery attached to one of the most sacred temples in all Japan. The master there was old and most wise. The young man begged an audience with the master, in hopes of being accepted as his pupil, to live and study with the great man.

"The young man—whose reputation had preceded him—was ushered into the master's chambers immediately. This was most unusual, and the young monk was greatly flattered.

"The master entered and they bowed to each other. They sat across a low table on the tatami mat floor and talked.

"The young man told the master of his journeys, of the teaching he had heard, of the monks he had 'bested' in his search for Truth. It was a most impressive tale. The master listened intently and acknowledged the young monk many times for his wit and intelligence.

"A teapot and cups were brought in, and the master began pouring tea for them both. The young man addressed the Master: 'I wish to remain here and study with you, for I sense that here, unlike with the others, there is much you have to offer me . . .'

"And all of a sudden, the young monk cried out in pain and alarm, jumping up from his place on the floor, shaking his robes and dancing about. The scalding hot tea had spilled all over his lap!

"The master sat calmly and continued pouring tea—which was overflowing the student's small cup and spilling out over the table onto the straw-matted floor where the young man had been sitting.

" 'What are you doing?!' the young monk demanded. 'I have been burned! Stop pouring! The cup is overflowing!'

" 'Go away from me, young man,' the master said. 'I have nothing to teach you. Your cup is too full . . . overflowing with all that you know and all that you think you don't know. Come back to me when your cup is empty and you are ready to receive what I have to give.' "

We sat in silence for a long time.

As I recall, it was the first time in a long time that there were no thoughts at all rattling around in my head.

I had stopped talking to myself.

Finally, he spoke up. "You want very much to be a success in Network Marketing, don't you?"

"Yes," I answered.

"You know some things about how to do this business—true?"

"Yes."

"And you know, too, that there are many things that you do *not* know about how to do this business—true?"

"Yes," I replied.

He sat up a bit, away from the back of the couch, and faced me directly as he spoke this next thought, carefully measuring out his words.

"There is nothing which you now *know*, and nothing about what you *think you don't know*, that will help you create the success you desire."

He paused for a moment, and continued.

"The key to your success lies only in *what you don't know that you don't know*. Do you understand?"

"No," I told him truthfully. "I have no idea what you're saying. How can I know what I don't even know that I don't know?"

"You can't," he said. "That's the secret."

CHAPTER FOUR

The Silver Screen

When I looked at my watch, it was a little past 1:00 A.M. We had been talking for almost six and a half hours. That is, I had been talking. As with our first meeting, he asked me question after question after question.

We spoke little or not at all about Network Marketing. The entire conversation had been about me—my past, present and future. And what was fascinating to me, was that I—who always watched the clock like a hawk—had no sense of the time passing.

Instead, I was left with a feeling of tremendous peace—and freedom. I was light—physically feeling younger than I had for years. It was as if all my worries, my anxieties about my circumstances and my doubts about the future had disappeared completely. I felt somehow more hopeful and very much alive.

Two parts of our conversation I shall never forget: we spoke about my "values" and my "life's purpose."

Throughout our talk, he would ask me if such and such were one of my *values*. At first, this question threw me. I wasn't sure what he meant.

He explained that *values*—as he was using the term—had to do with those essential qualities that were most important to me. And he used the example of *success*.

Success was certainly an important value of mine and I said so. Then he asked, "What does success mean to you?"

I said, "You know —"

"No, I don't know," he interrupted. "No one but you knows what success means *for you*. The best I can do would be to tell you what *I think* success means for you, and that's not the same thing. I'm interested in what *you* mean—not in what *I think* you mean."

Okay, I thought, and I took a deep breath and explained what success meant to me.

When I had finished, he summarized what I said: "So for you, success means being able to live your desires and dreams?"

I agreed.

"And what does success provide for you?" he asked.

I thought for a moment, then said, "Freedom."

"Good," he said. "Values come in pairs, one providing for the manifestation of the other. Just one by itself is incomplete . . . "

"Wait!" I interrupted. "You mean, always? Why in pairs?"

I suddenly felt a little self-conscious, as if I'd jumped in too impatiently. I think I actually blushed slightly. "Or, were you about to explain that?" I apologized.

He seemed to enjoy the interruption immensely. "Great question!" he beamed. "Let me answer it with another: Why did God tell Noah to bring two of each animal onto the Ark?"

The look of utter bewilderment on my face must have been quite comical—it drew a good-sized version of his trademark laughing explosion.

"Ah . . . ha . . . !" He wagged his finger instructively, like a professor making an important point—"We need another example, perhaps—a more practical one?" He continued, still chuckling. "Tell me: do you know why you have two eyes?"

"Bifocal vision . . . depth perception," I repeated from school-days memory.

"Right! *Very* good. It doesn't seem like we'd really *need* two, does it?—either eye works just fine on its own. But working together as a pair, they add to 'vision' the perception of 'depth.' And," and here he brought up the mock-professor finger again, "one eye 'anchors' the vision of the other—gives it a reference point.

"It's the same with your values. One supports the other. Together, they allow your vision to operate *in depth*."

I could grasp the poetry of this, but knew I didn't really understand what he was saying, and said so with my face.

"That's okay," he assured me. "Look at what you were just telling me. Do you see how 'success' and 'freedom' are interrelated for you?"

I replied that I did. I remember telling him how much of my life, I'd felt trapped . . . how without success, I felt like a prisoner.

"So you might say," he continued for me, "that 'success,'

for you, provides for the expression of 'freedom.' That the one actually gives the other a reference point, a context for its existence."

"Right, I see—they work together . . ." I was starting to get the sense of what he was saying—and it did truly feel like some sort of "sight" was being restored!

"My guess," he said, "is that you feel imprisoned to some extent about everything in your life. That's because your values of success and freedom are not being honored."

As we continued talking, I discovered other sets of values I had: appreciation and recognition . . . adventure and fun . . . communication and power . . . service and contribution . . . partnership and leadership . . . relationship and intimacy. There were others. These seemed the most important.

Then he asked, "What is your life purpose?"

That was the *biggest* question anyone had ever asked me.

What *was* my life purpose?

I didn't know and told him so.

"I want you to do something with me," he said. "It's a game I play when I want to know something, but just don't *get* it yet."

I agreed to play, and asked what I needed to do.

He told me to close my eyes, sit with my back fairly straight, rest my hands on my legs, and take a couple of long and slow, very deep breaths and relax as completely as possible.

I did.

Then he said, "What I want you to do now is to use your imagination. I want you to pretend that you're standing in front of a movie theater. There's a big crowd outside waiting to get in. You look up on the marquee and there, in huge letters, is your name, and it says, 'The True Story of His Incredible Life.'

"Go on in and take a seat."

I did.

Then he told me to imagine the lights dimming, the music coming up louder and the movie beginning on the screen.

He had me tell him all about the scenes I imagined on the screen. He kept asking questions about what was happening in the movie, pressing me for details of the events and people I was seeing. After a while, he stopped asking me questions and sat quietly, while I watched that movie of my life continue vividly before my eyes.

I have no idea how long it was before I opened my eyes. When I did, he was sitting there smiling at me. He asked, "Well, what was that like?"

"That was wild!" I replied. "I've never done anything like that in my life."

"Great," he said. "What happened?"

I described a number of scenes: some funny ones, a few sad ones (from when I was growing up)—and a whole bunch of things I'd never done before but that were in my movie anyway.

I was receiving an award in front of a hall full of people giving me a standing ovation . . . I was teaching or presenting to another group of people who were all tremendously moved by what I was saying . . . I'd written a book . . . There were many scenes of me traveling in far-off lands like Japan and China and Russia . . . It was astonishing how many different and wonderful things were there!

"How did it end?" he asked.

"It was funny," I told him. "It ended right here, right in this room. But instead of you sitting where you are now, I was sitting there. And there was a young woman sitting here where I am now, and I was asking her about her life's purpose."

He closed his eyes and we sat in silence for some time. Then, he looked at me and nodded his head up and down.

"So, what's your life purpose?" he asked again.

"Teaching," I said. "I'm a teacher . . . and a writer—and what I teach people is how to be successful and free. I show them how to achieve their life's purpose. And," I added, "I make a profound difference in thousands, even millions of people's lives."

I cannot tell you what an extraordinary sensation I experienced as I said those words.

CHAPTER FIVE

A Goal Bigger Than Winning

I spent that night in a guest room on the second floor above the Greatest Networker's office-study. It was quite late when we'd finished talking, and since he'd asked me to attend a training he was giving early the next morning, he invited me to stay the night. I hadn't brought a change of clothes, a razor or anything and was feeling a little awkward about that and told him so. He told me not to be concerned. He'd take care of it.

"Set your alarm so we can have breakfast together at seven. Be comfortable. Good night," he said as he left.

As I was about to get myself ready for bed, I realized with a start that I hadn't called my wife! By now it was well after 1:00 —she would be asleep. I felt a twinge of guilt at waking her up— but I knew it was better to wake her than have her worry.

I found a phone and called Kathy to let her know I wouldn't be home until the next day—that I was going to be an overnight guest of the Greatest Networker in the World!

I got her sleepy voice on the phone, and started to apologize right away. She stopped me—she hadn't worried, she said; she knew I was alright. In fact, she was *very* curious to know what had happened so far—which both pleased me and surprised me a little—and as sleepy as I was, I couldn't stop myself from recounting all my experiences of the past seven or eight hours in great detail. She was fascinated, and said she was very happy for me.

We hadn't talked like this in a long, long time.

Interesting . . . I thought, as I hung up the phone—that was a great connection *for Alaska*. Perhaps my wife wasn't the one of us who'd been so distant recently.

Now, thinking back over our call and all the things I'd said to her, I lay awake in my bed, reliving the day's events one more time. I finally drifted off during a scene in "The True Story of His Incredible Life," sitting in a front-row seat (not my "comfort zone" in the back!) of that movie theater. It was the scene where I was standing on stage in front of a whole room full of people . . . .

I woke up feeling more alert and happy than I'd been in years—first thing—*very* first thing. It was 5:30 when I looked at the clock!

The room was chilly. The window had been open all night, and from the sound of it, the birds were having an opportunity meeting in the trees right outside the cottage. I wrapped up in a robe I found in the closet and shivered happily as my feet tap-danced across the cold wood between the carpets that covered the floor. I opened the French doors, walked out onto the deck—and stopped dead in my tracks.

There, perched on the railing in front of me, were two huge and breathtakingly beautiful peacocks!

I'd never seen one so close up before, even in the zoo. The smaller of the two was almost pure white and didn't have much of a tail. But the big one (I guessed it to be a male) had tailfeathers that must have been six or seven feet long—at least! It was like the train of an ornate Chinese Imperial costume following and flowing out behind him.

The birds were far less startled by me than I was by them. They sat calmly on the wooden porch railing, moving their heads from side to side and tilting them, as if taking pictures of me from a variety of different angles. I felt a bit intimidated by them and slowly turned to withdraw back inside, when I heard a heavy *thunk*, followed by a rustling sound. I turned back again to see the big male—with full feathers spread out in a wide fan—doing a kind of fast back-and-forth two-step while "rattling his tail" at me. It was incredible.

I have no intimate knowledge of the habits and ways of peacocks. I wasn't sure whether he intended to attack me—or attempt to mate with me—or what. So, I chose to quickly acknowledge the animal verbally for having a magnificent bunch of feathers and backed promptly inside.

Just amazing.

I showered quickly and, wrapped again in my robe, went down the stairs.

There was a fire in the fireplace! On the couch was a bundle of clothes tied with a bright red yarn with a note on top. It said:

*Good morning. Here are some clothes and sneakers
for you. Hope they fit. Dial 22 from any phone if you
desire anything. See you at 7:00.*

Sneakers? For a training session?

I untied the clothes, which turned out to be a brightly colored warm-up/jogging suit with a white Ralph Lauren polo
shirt and gray rag-wool socks. This was going to be a unique
meeting, I thought.

I dressed, made the bed, and came back downstairs where I
rearranged the fire and added another couple of logs. I settled
into the couch nearest the fireplace after finding a little book
on *Peafowl: Breeding and Management.* At seven sharp, he
walked through the door carrying a large tray.

"Good day . . . good day. How are you?"

"Superb," I replied. "How are you?"

"Wonderful," he said. "Have you met Black and Mrs. Peal?"
he asked, pointing to the *Peafowl . . .* book next to me on the
couch.

"The peacocks?" I questioned—and then answered, "Yes, a
Black Shoulder male and female—peacock and peahen. How
old are they? I know he's at least five or so by the length of his
tail."

"You *are* quite the quick study," he said. "Black is 15 years
old. My guess on Mrs. Peal is, oh, perhaps two or three years
younger. From your reading you know they can live upwards
of 25 years and more."

"I've never been that close to one before. 'Beautiful' isn't
grand enough to describe them."

"Yes," he said, taking a deep and obviously satisfying breath.

"They are magnificent creatures. Walking flower gardens. Just being around them is a constant reminder for me of the awesome possibility of beauty in our lives—and of my relationship with that creation.

"Here's an animal," he went on, "that is simply *being* beautiful. They don't have to *do* anything. They *are* beauty. And what's more," he added, with a distinct twinkle in his eyes, "it's great fun being a person who 'has' peacocks." He made a motion towards the tray he'd set down in front of us. "Let's eat breakfast."

He uncovered a marvelous breakfast of fresh fruit, French toast and coffee for me. He simply had tea.

"You're not eating?" I asked after a rich, juicy taste of a kind of melon I didn't recognize.

"No," he said, "I rarely take breakfast. It slows me down. I have a couple of food supplements and one or two-too-many cups of tea. Sometimes, the family enjoys a big breakfast together, like on Sunday mornings, and I like that, too. But I don't usually eat breakfast, or lunch for that matter."

"Well," I inquired, "tell me about this training session."

He walked into his office and returned quickly with a small paperback book and tossed it to me. I caught it, turned it over and read the title out loud: *Coaching Kids To Play Baseball and Softball*.

"There are a number of fine books on how to do Network Marketing and training," he told me. "This is one of the best."

"*Coaching Kids . . . ?*" I asked, and I guess I clearly conveyed my disbelief.

"Yes," he replied. "*Coaching Kids . . .*

"When I was first learning how to do this business," he told me, "there weren't all the books and tapes we have today explaining how to do Network Marketing successfully. The only thing I knew was where *not to* look."

"What do you mean?" I asked.

"Network Marketing is a whole different paradigm of . . . —Do you know what a 'paradigm' is?"

"20 cents?" I quipped, and he paused, stared blankly at me for the briefest moment, and then exploded with deep-down, booming laughter.

"Great . . . that's great!" he exclaimed after he regained his breath. "*Pair o' dimes . . . 20 cents*. Exactly! You know how we say, 'Here's my two cents,' when we're giving someone our opinion or point of view? A paradigm is just that—a point of view, a way we see things.

"The paradigm of Network Marketing," he continued, as he stood up and walked around the couch and the room, "is so fundamentally different and distinct from all other paradigms of business, that it requires a pretty complete shift from the way we normally view business to appreciate and understand it.

"For example, in our industry, every single company, no matter how different its products and services are from any other's, competes directly with every other Network Marketing company in attracting people to their business opportunity. That kind of competition from every angle doesn't exist anywhere else—in any other industry. Do you see that?"

"Yes, I do," I said, nodding in agreement and following him with my eyes and ears as he paced round the room.

"Now, given that unique competitive environment, there is the tendency for individual distributors to offer their opportunity as *the best*. That's natural, but *how* they do that is critical.

"Sadly, most of them only think to accomplish creating the perception of 'best' based on their old paradigm values— being the best by putting *down* the competition. 'My dog's better than your dog.'

"That may be fine—when it's Ford versus GM," he continued, "or when multi-million-dollar fights for market share are being waged over the TV in the beer battles or cola wars. But when Network Marketing distributors put down other companies, they're also putting down the industry as a whole.

"What happens then—and remember, we are the 'word-of-mouth' business—is that there's this growing communication out there in the world about how bad this company is, and that company is, and this other company is.

"You want to hear an amazing statistic?" he asked.

I nodded yes.

"For every positive piece of word-of-mouth consumers pass around, there are 11 negative comments being shuttled about. Just think about that for a moment: for every positive thing that's said about you, your company or product, there are 11 negative things being said. Geometric progression works!—for us and against us, too. Soon, those 11 negatives become 22, then 44, and all the way up into the hundreds of thousands, as one person shares how bad Network Marketing is with another, and they tell five, and they tell five, etcetera.

"Do you see where I'm going with all of this?" he asked.

I did, and it was beginning to make me uncomfortable.

I remembered all the times I had told some prospect why

he or she didn't want to get involved with this other company or that one . . . that *my* company was really the only good Network Marketing company, the only one doing it *right*.

It had never occurred to me that this person might be thinking, "Why would I want to be involved in an industry where every company but one markets mediocre products, has an unfair compensation plan and treats their people poorly?!"

In fact, I was now beginning to feel a good-sized chunk of regret for all that negative talk I'd put out into the world.

"I see you know what I'm talking about," he said, obviously noticing my somber expression. "We all—every single Networking distributor—have the responsibility to 'sell' *our industry itself*, as well as our individual products and opportunity.

"Do you think it's the media who's responsible for the bad press about Network Marketing?" he asked.

"I did until this morning. Now, I think we are, all of us—I am," I answered ruefully.

"Yup," he said. "We are. Each one of us.

"Network Marketing is the ultimate in freedom," he continued, "the freest of all free enterprise. That's the front side. The back—the other side of the coin—is responsibility.

"Network Marketing is truly the *responsibility* business. We get paid for taking responsibility. The more of it we take on, the more we get paid. That's what the word 'sponsor' means— being responsible for the people you bring into the business.

"When you are responsible for an organization of thousands of people, you earn a lot of money. Which is great. That's as it should be.

"Now here's something interesting." He stopped pacing,

sat back down directly across from me and leaned forward.

"Right now, you are concerned with your survival in this business, with your responsibility for creating your own success—true?"

"Yes," I said.

"Okay. Now, what would be different if you were concerned about the success of the *entire* industry? If *that* were *your* responsibility?"

"Oh, wow . . . " I said, looking up at the ceiling. I brought my eyes back down and said, "Well, I probably wouldn't spend as much time focused on myself, that's for sure."

"What would you spend your time focused on?" he asked.

"Making sure people knew the good news about Network Marketing and thought really well of us. Getting the word out. Helping people understand how great this is. Getting rid of abuses in the industry—you know, front-loading and crazy earnings claims. Things like that," I said.

"Would you be at all concerned about whether somebody said 'Yes' or 'No' to trying your products or joining your opportunity?"

"No. I wouldn't."

"And would that allow you to approach building your business differently than the way you've been doing it?"

"Yeah. It *really would*," I said. Boy, this was interesting! I actually experienced what people mean when they talk about *seeing the light*. I'd just seen it.

"*I got it!*" I exclaimed. "By taking my focus and attention off myself, and putting it on something bigger, *much* bigger, the problems I now think are big get smaller—immediately. They seem so simple now. I don't care about them anymore."

"Bingo!" he said. "Success Secret Number Thirty-Six Revealed . . . " and he laughed. "Have a goal bigger than you are. The bigger the better. That way, you don't have time to sweat the small stuff. And the bigger your goal, the more everything else becomes small stuff . . . "

He brought his hands together and touched the tips of his fingers to his lips thoughtfully, taking a long breath and letting it out.

"Boy, I really got off into that one." He sat back into the couch and took a long taste of his tea. "Do you remember where we were before I got started on all of that?

"— Oh, I know," he said, interrupting himself. "You asked about the book *Coaching Kids* . . . and how come I recommended it as a good book on Network Marketing. Isn't it nice to have a memory?" He seemed amused by his own question, which was clearly rhetorical.

"Early on," he said, "I began to look for the knowledge in places outside of traditional or conventional business, because I knew how unique Network Marketing really was. I was searching for some specific new material about how to teach and train my Network. That's how I discovered what kids' sports had to teach us about building a Networking business.

"Here," he said, gesturing for me to hand him the *Coaching* . . . book, which was in front of me on the table. "Let me read you something."

I handed him the book, and he turned a couple of pages and began reading aloud.

> *We believe that the objects of youth sports on all
> levels are fun, learning, individual development, and
> winning—in that order.*
>
> *We make no secret of our feeling that the most
> important part of your job as coach is to make sure
> your squad has fun; the second most important part
> is to teach them all you can; the third, to make sure
> they develop as individuals and members of a team;
> and fourth, to win when you can.*
>
> *We're not suggesting that you overlook the impor-
> tance of succeeding and winning—the coach who for-
> gets to encourage the kids to strive as hard as they can
> to win is cheating his team. But learning to enjoy the
> game is more important.*

He put the book down and set his eyes on mine in that
intense way of his.

"That's a perfect description of the role of the Sponsor in
Network Marketing," he said. "It's another example of how
different this business is from conventional enterprises.

"Number one—to coach your people to have fun. Number
two—to teach them the skills they need to succeed. Three—
to help them develop and grow, first as individuals, then as
members of a team. And number four—to win . . . when you
can.

"And I promise you," he said earnestly, "if you do one, two
and three, then you will always win—*always.*"

CHAPTER SIX
Teaching Kids Teaching

As we drove out to the place where the training session was to take place, I asked him what it was like when he began in Network Marketing.

"The first couple of years I was in this business," he told me, "I experienced only a little success—*at best*.

"I started off like gangbusters. I made up a 'names list' of 250 people. I sent them all a terrific four-page letter I'd written, included some background articles on the products and their ingredients, along with some reprints I'd come across on health and nutrition, and included a sample of the products for them to try. What a great letter!

"209 of them said 'Yes' and ordered the product—and I signed up 50 of them as distributors. Not bad, huh?" he said, turning quickly to look at me with a broad smile.

"Not bad at all," I said.

"Trouble was," he continued, "after four or five months, not one of them—*not one*—was doing the business!"

"Really?" I questioned. "What happened?"

"What happened," he told me, "was that what I was doing was working beautifully. *For me*. And not for them.

"I thought I was really good," he continued, "but in this business, 'good' doesn't count. What counts is being duplicatable. Which is precisely what I was *not*.

"I'd had a background in advertising and marketing, so getting people to see value in my products and having them want to try them was easy for me. I'd been doing that for years. Plus, I had a reputation for appreciating quality and having integrity. So my friends and associates trusted me. They assumed that if I thought the products were worthwhile, they were—so they'd try them, too. And our products were good— *very good*.

"In fact—" he was really warming to his subject, and seemed to be relishing the memory of his early "success"—"I could persuade just about *anyone* to try the products—and I could excite many of them to come into the business, too.

"The one thing that was missing," he said, "was doing the business in a way that others could easily do, too. The only way I knew how to do the business was *my* way—and hardly anybody else could do that.

"I was a marketing expert—they weren't. And for 20 years I'd been involved in natural health and nutrition—most of them hadn't. So although I was successful, individually, I wasn't able to give my people a simple, easy way to duplicate my success. The only way they could have done that was *to be just like me*."

"So, what did you do?" I asked.

"So, what did I do?" he parodied good-naturedly. "So, I

failed!" He punctuated the punchline with another one of his huge laughs and slapped his knee.

It was clear that he'd told this story more than once—and that for him, it got better every time.

In fact, he was laughing so hard, he pulled the truck off to the edge of the road for a moment, pushed his glasses up with his hands and wiped the tears from his eyes, continuing to laugh at himself and shake his head all the while.

"Ahh me, this is such a wonderful, glorious business," he laughed. "It's so beautifully simple and straightforward." He steered the truck back onto the road and continued.

"That was my first big lesson in Network Marketing. Once I realized what was missing in my approach, I set out to find a way to do this business that *anyone*—of no matter what age, experience, background, talents or whatever—could do. And more importantly, what anyone could *teach other people to do* easily and effortlessly.

"And for that, I found that the kids were some of my best mentors."

Ah, so that's where the kids come in, I mused.

Just then, we pulled into a parking lot behind a Little League ball field across the road from a sprawling red brick elementary school. "Come on," he said. "Your trainers are waiting for you."

* * *

I spent the next hour and a half watching and playing tee-ball with 15 six- and seven-year-old kids—13 boys and two girls.

We didn't have tee-ball when I was growing up. Here, there's no pitching; the kids get to hit a ball that sits still, perched on top of a telescoping rubber stand much like a very tall golf tee attached to home plate. And we didn't have girls on our Little League team, either—and certainly not short-stops with arms like slingshots who also hit line drives that made the fielders fall to the ground ducking to get out of the way!

The kids had a great time. So did I. And the very first thing they did in their practice blew me away.

All the kids sat around on the bottom rail of the backstop, behind home plate. The Greatest Networker enthusiastically called out each one by name.

"Here's the Hornets' ace shortstop, Julie Dugan!" he announced. Then Julie got up, ran out to home plate and took off her cap, waving it high in the air, and all the other kids clapped, whistled and cheered, and shouted out her name. Then he called out the next player, then the next . . .

They began their practice *cheering for each other*. That was it. Amazing.

Throughout the whole thing, the Greatest Networker was an almost endless stream of praise, constantly telling the kids how great they did.

Well, actually, he'd ask them first. "How'd ya do?" Then he'd acknowledge them for noticing how they did; and *then* he'd tell them how good they were.

I also noticed that all his praise was focused on how much they were *improving* over the week before, or even the year before.

When they messed up (which they did a lot), he'd stop

what was going on and ask them, "What happened?" Most of the time, the kid who goofed would say, "I did this or did that," and the Greatest Networker/coach would ask, "What could you do differently next time?"

Sometimes the kids didn't know what they'd done; then he'd ask, did anyone else know what happened? When he got an answer to that one, he'd ask the kid him- or herself if that were true—and what was a different way they could do it next time?

At first this whole process seemed a little strange to me, asking the kids everything. It actually struck me as kind of phony. Why not just tell them? It would sure save time. Besides, I thought, he already knew why—so why ask them?

So, I pulled him aside, and asked him about that.

"What do you learn when you ask me a question and I tell you the answer?" he asked me.

I thought about that, then replied, "I learn the answer."

"Exactly," he said. "And of what use is that?"

"Well, then I know what to do," I said.

"And of what use is that?" he asked.

"Once I know what to do, I can do it," I replied.

"Yes," he said, "you *can* do it—but *do you?*"

"No, not always. Actually, not often," I had to admit. Knowing the answer and doing something about it seemed very different.

"Two things are important here," he told me.

"First, when you arrive at the answer yourself, it's very different than when someone else tells it to you. Its meaning is deeper, and there isn't any question about whether or not the other person is correct. It's *your* answer. You own it. And you're much more likely to remember it when you find yourself in a similar situation again.

"What's more," he continued, "when you discover the answer for yourself, you not only get the answer you were seeking, but you get trained in finding answers. So, there's twice the benefit.

"*Knowing* the answer, *having* the answer, is a far cry from *doing* the answer—would you agree?"

"Yes, I see," I said.

"But the real secret is *being* the answer. Do you know what I mean by that?"

"No," I said, "not really."

"Okay," he said. "Let's say I've got a little guy here who's learning how to hit a ball for the first time. So I tell him how to hold the bat, where to place his hands, how to stand, and I tell him the way to swing properly . . . I give him all the information there is to know about hitting a baseball. Now—does he know how to do it?"

"Yes," I said, "but I can see that knowing all that doesn't mean he *can* do it, and it certainly isn't *doing* it."

"Good," he said. "Yes, he *knows* how. He's *got* the information about it, and information is really great to have. But he isn't *doing* it—yet.

"And here's the other step: he may *do* it once or twice, but he isn't necessarily a hitter—yet. Being a hitter is just that—*being* a hitter."

He must have sensed my struggle with his terminology—it sounded a bit like his verbs were getting twisted around each other. I felt my mind quipping a quick satire of my puzzled

thoughts—"How do you *do* a *being* of *having* what you *know*
. . . ?" and remembered that gloriously circular book title, *What
You Don't Know That You Don't Know* . . .

He interrupted my thoughts to explain. "Have you ever
heard anyone talk about goal-setting with the terms, 'Have
. . . Do . . . Be . . . ?' *Have* the things you want to have . . . *Do*
the things you want to do . . . *Be* the kind of person you want
to be . . . ?"

I nodded that I had.

"The way I've found that works best is to focus on *being*
first. Once you achieve that, *doing* and *having* come naturally.
If you approach it the other way around, you can spend a lifetime *not* accomplishing your goals. *Being* first is actually easier,
because *being* begins in your mind. Anybody can *be* anything,
anytime he or she wants."

I confess, that didn't completely clear it up for me—and I
knew that he knew that.

"Well, I know one thing," I ventured. "We're *doing* talk
about this, but I'm also keeping you from *being* a Little League
coach."

"Right you are!" He seemed amused and delighted that I'd
taken a stab at knowing what I was talking about. "I'd like to
talk some more with you about *being* and *accomplishing*—but
let's have a conversation about that after practice. Okay?"

And back we went to join our "trainers."

Chapter Seven
Asking Right Questions

After we'd said goodbye to the kids—almost all of whom thanked me for coming and asked if I'd be back next week to help out, which I must say made me feel really terrific— and climbed into his truck, I asked anxiously about *being* and *accomplishing*.

He held up his hand and interrupted me, "Not so fast. We'll do that. But first, tell me—did you have fun?"

"I sure did," I exclaimed.

"That's great," he said. "Did you learn anything new?"

"Did that too," I said.

"What?" he asked.

"That thing you did in the beginning, when you had them all come up to the plate as you called out their names like a ballpark announcer and everybody cheered and applauded— that was amazing. I loved it! What a great way to start."

"We did that at our very first practice of the season," he told me. "It gets the kids off to a great beginning. They're a success right off the bat, and it makes them all feel special—they're all stars immediately."

He went on, "And did you notice how the parents stick around for that?"

I hadn't 'til he mentioned it, but it was true. All the mothers and fathers had stood there behind the backstop, and they'd cheered and clapped, too.

"Anything else?" he asked me.

"A bunch," I said. "The whole business of *asking* the kids what they did, rather than *telling* them—I got a lot from that. I remember my favorite teachers in school: they were the ones who let me discover things on my own, just like you were doing—"

"And the others?" he inquired.

"The others? Oh—you mean my other teachers . . . the ones who told me 'do this' or 'do that,' or just had us repeat and remember? I was bored to death in their classes."

"Hmm . . . which kind first taught you about higher math and computers?" he wondered aloud. He must have been remembering what I'd told him about my "pioneering" passion for hacking in those early computer days. I knew he already knew the answer.

"The first kind. Mr. Dougherty, my eleventh-grade math teacher. I remember his face—and his voice—as clear as yesterday."

"Right," was his only comment, followed by, "Go on."

"Let's see . . . the way you praised the kids—the way you had them acknowledge themselves first. It seems to me that that gives the kids responsibility for themselves, for relying on their own ideas first. That was just great."

I thought back to find a good example. Truth was, there were lots to pick from.

"Who was the little boy on second base, the one who cried when he got confused about whether to call time or throw the ball to first?"

"Johnny."

"Yeah, Johnny—the way you talked with him was terrific."

"Thanks," he said, pleased at the acknowledgement. "What did you get from that?"

"Well, I noticed how you brought his attention *off* how he was feeling without even dealing with it directly. First thing you did was kneel down, so you were on his level. Then you just asked him, 'What happened?' He told you that some kids were yelling, 'Throw to first,' while others were shouting, 'Call time,' and he didn't know what to do. You asked, 'What do *you* think would have been best?' And he said, 'Call time,' and you said, 'Okay, let's do the play over and see if that works.' Then you did, and he called time, and it worked great. That was incredible."

"So, what did you get from that?"

"I just told you," I said.

"No," he corrected gently, "you just gave me a description of what I did. I asked, What did you *get* from that? In what way did that contribute something to you?"

"Oh," I said. "Well, I saw how I don't have to be controlled by my feelings about something. That it works better to focus on *what happened* and do something about that."

I looked over at him to see his response. He just looked at the road and said, "Good!" Then he asked, "And tell me, what results did *you* get?"

"Results? How do you mean?"

"Results," he repeated. "What results did you achieve out there today?"

"Well . . ." I thought for a moment, "I showed Justin—was that his name?"

He nodded.

"I showed Justin how to hold his hand so that he could catch the ball without it scooting out of his glove: fingers up when the ball came at him above his waist, and fingers down when the ball came to him below his waist. That way, he wouldn't miss the play, or get hit in the face with the ball."

"That's great," he laughed. "So, you had fun . . . you learned something new . . . and you got results, too—right?"

"Yes," I said. "I did."

"Congratulations—you win!"

Win at what? I wondered—and then I remembered the points from the *Coaching Kids* . . . paperback: fun, learning, growth and development—and winning, when possible. Click.

"Those are the three ingredients in accomplishment," he told me. "You get results. You learn, develop and grow. And, you have fun. All three are required. If any one is missing, you don't have real accomplishment."

"I see that," I said excitedly, "I really do! I've done things where I've gotten results and learned something new, but didn't have much fun. And I've done things where I had fun, but didn't learn or get the result I was after. That's wonderful. Accomplishment is all three."

"Yup," he said. "All three."

"And," he continued, "that's why you don't want to focus on just results—with yourself *or* with your people . . ." Aha! I thought—so this really *is* Network Marketing—and I flashed on the scene in the movie *Karate Kid*, where the master teaches his student karate by having him wax a car all day long: "Wax on, wax off, wax on, wax off . . . "

" . . . If you do," the Networker/coach was saying, "you might get the *results*, but not really accomplish anything. This is vital in building a Network Marketing business: No results—no check. No learning—you get left behind. No fun—you quit, or burn out, or burn out *and* quit."

"I see that," I said, shaking my head. It all seemed so simple and so easy as he explained it, and I told him so.

"That's because it's just information," he confided. "Once you start *being* that way . . . once you begin to *be* accomplishing, then you'll *do* those things accomplishing people do, and you'll *have* those things accomplishing people have."

"So, how do I *accomplish* that?" I asked.

"That," he exclaimed with emphasis, "is the $64,000 *a month* question!"

"Do you know the answer?" I asked, *very* tentatively.

"Yes," he replied.

"Will you tell me?" I begged.

"Yes," he said.

Silence . . .

For too long . . .

"*When?*" I pleaded.

He slowed the truck down, turned to me and made an exaggerated face with his eyebrows arched way up, and his eyes as wide as could be—and then he said, in an itsy-bitsy cartoon voice, "Can I tell ya now, mister? Huh, can I . . . can I . . . *please?*"

[57]

I think we both laughed for two minutes solid.
What an amazing man he was.

CHAPTER EIGHT

The Habit of Being You

B eing, that's what we were going to talk about next.

But I had to wait a bit before we'd get into it. And what a wait! I know that I keep saying, "Amazing!" but I was being blown away left and right by everything about this guy. I was seeing things, and doing things, saying and listening to things I'd never experienced before in my life. Heck, I'd never *dreamed* about most of this. Yet, here it was—here *I* was.

It really was all pretty *amazing!*

As we climbed out of the truck back at his house, he turned to me and asked, "Want to freshen up?"

I said, "Sure."

And he asked, "Have you ever had a Japanese bath?"

"No," I told him truthfully. "At least I don't think I have."

"Oh, you'd remember," he assured me. "Come on. You're in for a treat."

"It's my opinion," he said as we walked into the main house, "that the Japanese are eating our lunch in business, simply because they know about baths and we don't. I'm on a one-man crusade to establish *the bath* in America, so the United States can regain our position as the world leader."

He turned and looked at me. "I'm not kidding!" he said with an earnest smile.

The inside of the house was just as magnificent as the grounds and his office-study, although a bit more formal. It was a truly gracious interior—light and airy, filled with lush plants and fresh-cut flowers. Somehow, I felt, it would always be summer in these rooms.

Some of the pieces of furniture were really extraordinary. Antiques, big time! As we passed the wide entrance to the living room, I glanced in casually—*and stopped dead in my tracks!*

He had walked on ahead of me, but when he noticed I'd stopped, he turned back and asked, "What?"

"Tha . . . that," I stammered. "Is that what I think it is?"

"Is what what you think it is?" he asked as he returned beside me.

There, above the mantle, *in this man's private home*, in a magnificent, gilded, splendidly ornate period frame, about six feet wide and more than four feet tall, *was a Monet!* Obviously, not a copy—an original! My mind literally reeled—in fact, I think my legs did, too.

"*That's a M-monet!*" I exclaimed. "Water-lilies . . . it's from the water lil . . . oh, what were they called?"

"*Nymphéas*," he replied. And then he let loose with one of those booming laughs of his—the biggest one I'd heard yet.

He threw his arm around my shoulder and gave me a *very* strong hug, laughing all the while.

"I do like you!" he said between trying to catch his breath and recover from his all-consuming laughter. It took a good half-minute.

"Ahha," he gasped, bringing himself together. "No, no. It's not a Monet. It's a *Me*. I painted it. But thank you *so much!* That was wonderful!"

I shook my head, again in disbelief—and again, amazed.

As we continued walking through the house—it was a *big* house—he told me that he had gone to art school, even had a Bachelor of Fine Arts degree, and although he'd never painted anything of real consequence before, it was something he'd always dreamed of doing. That painting had been one of his goals for a long, long time. 20 years, he told me.

Monet was the artist he loved most. After he became successful in Network Marketing—successful enough, he said, so that he had the time to do the things he'd always wanted to do, but hadn't yet done—he'd purchased a whole bunch of books and prints of Monet's paintings. He'd studied them, and then set out to paint his own work in a style close to Monet's.

He'd succeeded more than admirably. His painting looked like a museum piece and I told him so.

"Thanks," he said, appreciatively. "I think, when I die, I'll look back on my kids and that painting as my greatest contributions."

And then he added, like Teddy Roosevelt charging San Juan Hill—"*To the bath!*"

The bath room—which in this case had nothing to do with being a toilet—was remarkable, as I expected.

It was walled and ceilinged in wide-plank, highly polished, dark red cedar boards. What wasn't wood, was glass—two huge glass skylights and a large glass window that extended the whole width of the room. The room was filled with a number of monster-sized and lush green hanging ferns and ivy.

The entrance to the room was a small foyer with benches and hooks for hanging our clothes. He told me that the bath was traditionally done in the nude, by men and women alike—but if I minded, I could have a bathing suit and he'd wear one as well.

I said that I was a purist at heart, and I'd do it as it was meant to be done.

The first half of the bath room floor was covered with closely placed cedar slats, with a sub-floor and drain beneath. There were two tubs: one was raised up (and steaming!) about three feet high, and the other was set into the flooring, square shaped—made of marble, I thought—and probably about three or more feet deep.

Part of the floor was a rock garden, similar to those in pictures I'd seen of those tranquil Zen temples in Japan. The sand was raked in straight lines and swirling patterns. It was not the kind of place on which you put your foot.

He motioned me to sit down on one of the small stools that was facing the wall off to the side of the taller tub.

On the wall were two sets of hot and cold water taps; one had a central spigot, and the upper one had a showerhead attached to the wall by a snaking, flexible hose. Beside the stools were wooden buckets that held probably about a gallon of water. Each had a kind of crude, hand-made ladle inside.

He filled his bucket up with warm water from the tap on the wall, dumped it over his head two or three times, and told me to do the same. Then he picked up one of those natural sponges, squeezed some clear liquid soap from a tall white bottle and tossed the bottle over to me. He began to soap himself all over with the sponge.

"It's interesting that we Westerners climb into the tub first," he said, "then we soap ourselves. The Japanese taught me to do it the other way 'round. They have a number of reasons for that. It saves water—you don't have to keep filling up the bathtub with fresh water all the time. And knowing the Japanese, I'm sure it also has to do with being respectful of other people, and of the water as well. After all, only a Gaijin, oblivious and disrespectful of other people, and of the water as well, would get into a tub all dirty."

"*Gaijin* . . . ?" I wondered aloud.

"*Gaijin* means 'foreigner' in Japanese," he told me, "but in my opinion, the essential translation is *barbarian*. The Japanese *really* think that they are the most refined culture on Earth—and that all foreigners are barbarians," he laughed, "especially Americans."

"And with good reason," he added. "We don't bathe nearly often enough."

When he had finished soaping from head to toe, he filled up his bucket again and rinsed himself off at least a dozen times. I did the same.

Then he stood up, and said, "Now, a Japanese bath is *very* hot. Much hotter than you are probably used to."

"I like hot baths," I protested.

"Please, trust me," he insisted, "this is *very hot*. I suggest that you use the shower and make it as hot as you can stand it by turning the temperature up gradually. Then you'll be able to come and sit in the tub."

I said that I'd really like to try the tub directly. He shook his head and smiled. Said "Be my guest," and stood aside with a gallant gesture of his arm, as I walked up, climbed to the side of the tub and stuck my foot in.

No sooner had I done that, than I pulled my leg back *out* as fast as possible!

He just looked at me—no expression.

"I think . . . I'll do . . . as you suggested," I admitted, sheepishly waiting for his *I told you so*.

It never came. He just said, "Good," and went over and sat slowly, almost reverently down in the tub. The water came all the way up to his neck.

After I'd come as close as I could tolerate to scalding myself with the shower, I joined him in the tub. Boy, it was *hot!* But the shower helped a lot. At least now I could stand to get in and sit down inside the tub.

"Don't move," he told me. "The trick is to sit stone still 'til you get used to it."

Slowly, I adjusted to the temperature. I had closed my eyes and fought the heat at first. Now, I was being melted—literally—into a state of peace and pleasure.

When I finally opened my eyes, I saw my friend had leaned his head all the way back on the edge of the tub, and draped a hot washcloth over his face.

I looked around. The whole room was filled with a light, steaming mist coming from the hot tub. I imagined he probably didn't want to talk at that moment, but I mustered the courage to ask quietly if he was willing to tell me about *being*.

He slowly removed the cloth from from his face and smiled a deeply satisfied smile. "Sure," he said, took a deep breath and began—as usual, with a question.

"Who are you?"

Great, I thought, another easy one. I was silent for a long time. I knew just saying my name wouldn't do. He'd just ask me another question. So, I waited and thought about the question some more.

After a small-scale eternity, I said, "I'm the sum total of all the experiences I've ever had . . . all I've thought about me and those experiences . . . and all anybody's ever told me about me and them."

His eyes blinked open wide with a start. And to my delight, this time, he was the one who said . . .

"Amazing." I wasn't sure whether he was speaking to me or to himself. "I honestly did not expect that answer. That's wonderful!"

I must say, whether it was the anesthesia of the bath or just the joy of hearing those complimenting words coming from him, I did feel quite *wonderful* at that moment.

"Thanks," I said, uncharacteristically forgetting to preface my gratitude with *Gosh*.

"Very good," he said, with genuine enthusiasm, now clearly addressing me. "And do you know what all of that—your thoughts and the thoughts of others about you—adds up to?"

"My being?" I asked and answered at the same time.

"Close," he said. "It's what your sense of your being *comes from* . . . what creates how you *be* in any situation. It adds up to your habits of belief. What some people call your *belief systems.*

"I don't say 'belief *systems*,' just because I don't think people really understand that term. Most people think 'systems' are so complicated that they're powerless to change them. Besides, I maintain that our beliefs are *habits of thought* we have. And because they *are* simply habits, we know how we got them—and how to change them, too.

"Habits," he continued, "are things we think or do without conscious attention . . . without being aware of them. The moment we are aware of what we are thinking or doing, it's no longer a habit. It's a choice.

"So, can you see, we can change our habits by making conscious choices?" he asked.

"Yes," I said, and I did see that very clearly.

"So," he continued, "we have these habits of belief about ourselves, and the reason they are so important is that they control what we have, do and be in our lives."

We were back at "have, do and be," and my face must have shown that I was still not on solid ground here.

"Let me give you an example," he said.

"I grew up fat. When I graduated from high school, I weighed 250 pounds."

"Really?" I exclaimed. "Well, you're not fat now . . . and I bet you'll be a whole lot thinner after this bath!"

"Quite true!" he nodded, laughing with me. "But seriously, although I've actually weighed around 175 for years, I spent much of that time still *believing I was fat.*

"You see, for almost 30 years, my experience had given me all the evidence I needed to see myself as 'fat.' What's more, other people were quite willing to contribute to that evidence. And so was I! Every chance I got, whether I knew it or not, I would simply add to that belief by . . . *believing it* some more! My mind had gotten the 'I am fat' message literally thousands of times.

"In school, I was the brunt of fat jokes and lots of cruelty about being fat. When I first lost a good chunk of weight, I bought slimmer pants that were really much too tight for me. Now, I thought I was doing that because I was glorying in finally being thinner, finally being able to fit into a smaller size. Then one day I realized that in fact, by buying pants that were too small and having my belly bulge out over my belt— I was continuing to live out my belief that I was fat!

"Later on, after I'd lost over 75 pounds, I'd mention something about being fat, and people would be shocked. They'd tell me how great I looked, how thin. And it took years of that kind of input, but eventually I began to replace my habit of believing I was fat with one where I truly believed I was, at last, thin.

"That whole process took *more than 15 years!*"

He closed his eyes and visibly shuddered. "What a waste," he said.

He was silent for some time. Then, he took a very deep, slow breath, and opened his eyes as he let the air slowly escape his lungs.

"The Buddhists teach that life is suffering," and his voice was filled with a powerful emotion. "And I agree—to a point. What they do not teach, however, is how darn unnecessary it is. *Being* suffering, *being* anything, can be changed, if we literally put our minds to it. We only need to change our minds. And we do *that* all the time. We just have to learn how to do it on purpose.

"I believe that's what Christ was teaching when he said, 'Turn to him the other cheek.' He was telling us, 'Resist not evil'; just change your mind.

"Habits of belief are created the same way as any other habits—simply by doing the same thing over and over until you don't think about it any more. That means, you can create a new habit the very same way, just as I did when I replaced my fat belief habit with a thin one. I just changed my mind.

"Now, when I first did this, I was unaware of what I was doing. I didn't see how the 'thin talk' I'd begun to hear from others—and from myself—was changing my habit of belief that I was fat.

"Think of it as a balance scale in our minds. One side is weighted down with all the talk and experiences that make up our predominant habits of belief. But we can change that, simply by adding enough 'weight' to the other side as we create new habits. Do you see what I'm talking about?" he asked, holding his hands out in front of him, palms up, moving up and down like the two sides of the scale.

I did. And I said so.

"Okay," he said. "So, if you accept what I've said so far as if it were true, what's the first question you've got?"

"How do you change the habit?"

"Replace it with a new one."

"How?"

"How'd you get the original?" he asked, then answered the question himself. "You got it by having a thought about what you believed. Then another. Then another, and another and another. Pretty soon, you didn't have to add any more thoughts—your habit of belief was in place. You just kept it there, sustained it, reinforced it, every time you added some new input—some experience, something you said about that, something someone else said to you about it—that agreed with or could be added to that existing habit of belief."

"So," I said, "you begin replacing your existing habit of belief—what did you call it, dominant . . . predominate?"

"Predominant," he offered.

"Right. So you begin replacing your predominant habit of belief by adding new thoughts to the other side of the scale. Right?"

"Right," he agreed. "What kind of thoughts?"

"Thoughts which are about the new belief you want to have."

"YES!" he shouted, and jumped up out of the tub.

He turned to me like someone exaggerating a symphony orchestra conductor with his arms moving back and forth to some grand unheard marching music, and he pointed his fingers at me as he spoke, keeping the imaginary beat with his words:

"And . . . so . . . " (Point, point.)

"I . . . say . . . that . . . you . . . " (Point, point, point, point.)

"Have . . . the . . . habit . . . " (Point, point, point.)

"Of . . . being . . . HOT!" (Point, point, POINT!)

"Well come on," he laughed. "We'll change that one right now!" And before he'd finished saying "right now," he'd jumped into the other tub, where he ducked completely under the water, and stayed there.

After a good 10 seconds or so, he shot up out of the water with a great *whoosh*, exclaiming, "Whup, whup, whooa! Yes! YES!

"Come on. *Get in here!*" he demanded as he jumped out.

I did as I was told. It was freezing! The entire tub was pure ice—no, colder. It was below zero!

"*Whhhaaa!*" I screamed out and jumped out at the same time. As I rubbed the water from my eyes he threw a towel at me.

"Great, huh?" I think he was asking me, but I wasn't very clear about it. All I remember at that moment was me jumping around and squeaking, "Ooh . . . Ooh . . . Ooh . . . !"

"Wow!" I said. I hadn't done that since boys' camp. "Wow!" I said again. "Wheew!"

"How do you feel?" he asked, having just finished toweling himself off, wrapping the towel around his middle and tucking it in.

"Great!" I said. "It feels *invigorating*. Do you do this often?" I asked.

"Every day," came the reply. "I can't think of anything better for your body—or for your mind. I'm actually 97 years old. How do I look?" And he laughed another of his boomers—only this one seemed deeper by an octave or two.

"You look great, *old man*," I quipped back.

"Hey," he said, as if remembering something special, "would you like to meet my family?"

"You bet!" I said enthusiastically. "I'd wondered about where they were."

"Me too," he laughed. "I haven't seen them since yesterday afternoon, before you arrived. Let's go find them."

CHAPTER NINE
Housekeeper Master

As we left the Japanese bath and entered the small dressing foyer, I noticed that the clothes we had worn were gone. In their place were two neatly folded piles of clothing. One was my my own which I'd worn on Friday, now clean as new!

I began to dress. My friend had just put on a faded denim work shirt and then he unfurled what looked to be a big scarf or a shawl.

Odd, I thought. "What's that?" I asked, pointing to the large piece of brightly printed fabric he was holding.

"It's a *sarong*," he said. "They wear them in Thailand and tropical islands, like Java and Bali."

"It's beautiful," I commented.

"Thanks," he said. "They are the single most comfortable garment in the world," he added. "Want to try one?"

"Ah, sure," I said, a little hesitantly. "How do you wear it?"

He walked over to some drawers that were built into the

wall and pulled out a bright blue bolt of cloth with a white and darker blue embroidered border.

"You're a blue person—aren't you?" he asked.

"Am I?" I replied, with some curiosity.

"Your clothes . . ." he said, pointing to my pile on the bench, " . . . are all blue."

They were. I was a blue person all right.

He showed me two different ways of tying the sarong. I chose the one I liked best, which was different than the way he had his. He'd just pulled his around himself and tied a knot in the front. The way I wore mine seemed more, well, conservative. More formal.

Following his careful instructions, I wrapped it around me once, held the two ends off to the side, pinched the two sides of cloth which were closest to my body tight together, made a couple of back and forth folds, tucked them back into the whole thing, and folded the waist down all around.

I can't imagine that anyone would understand all of this based on that description. It's one of those things, like tying a necktie, that you've got to *do* yourself to get how it works.

As we were walking back through the house, I asked, "How did our clothes get there? I didn't hear anybody come in."

"Probably, Rachel—that's my wife. But it could have been Rebecca—that's my daughter. Or Kazuko. She's the woman who takes care of us."

"*Kazuko.*" I repeated the name just to hear myself say it. "That's Japanese, too?"

"Yes," he laughed. "You've noticed my love for things Japanese!

"Kazuko-san is a joy. But she's a very difficult woman," he said, and I couldn't tell whether he was serious or not. He must have noticed what I was thinking, because he added in mock protest, "It's true. You'll see."

We walked into the living room with that marvelous MLMer-Monet over the mantle, and he told me to "Sit," while he went over to a huge French country wardrobe kind-of-thing, spread the doors open wide and did something I couldn't see. I guessed that was where his stereo was kept—as the music filled the room.

Amazing, I thought. "Country music?" I asked.

"A man of many tastes and talents," he answered. "Pop quiz: who's singing?" he asked me.

"Ah . . . hmmm, Emmylou Harris?" I asked, guessing the name of probably the only woman I was certain sang country music.

"Good guess," he said, peering out from around the door of the wooden cabinet. "K. T. Oslin."

Well, I'm no big fan of country music. More so by ignorance than by choice. I'd never listened to it much. I figured it was for a different kind of person than me. I know that sounds silly, but that's what I'd thought—'til then, at least. Frankly, K. T. Whomever-she-was was pretty good.

What a trip, I thought: Stereo's hidden away in French country antiques, mock-Monet on the wall, just come from a Japanese bath, sitting here in a *sarong*, listening to country music . . . Talk about "Stranger In A Strange Land." I loved it!

"Ah, Gaijin-san . . . no lock an' lorr today? But I rike it so much!" said a strange new voice from the other side of the room.

I turned to see a small Japanese woman, with her extra-long, straight black hair pulled back in a ponytail—and dressed in a brightly colored warm-up suit, no less—bowing to me, her hands on her thighs. She leaned forward and smiled. I had absolutely no idea how old she was—30, 35, maybe more, maybe even less. There wasn't a line or wrinkle on her lovely face.

"Oh, oh," said my host, as he closed the doors to the wardrobe and turned to face the woman. She danced down the steps and marched over to me in long strides, almost bounds, which I never would have expected from such a demure Oriental woman. Stuck out her hand and said, "Hello. I'm Kazuko. It's a pleasure to meet you." And this time, there was *no hint* of an accent of any kind!

I said Hi, and added that it was a pleasure to meet her, as well. For a moment I felt I was groping for words. "Ah—were you the person who set my clothes out for me?" I asked her.

"Like a ninja—right. Sneaking around, lighting fires, delivering clothes," she said and laughed with twinkling eyes. I liked her right away.

"So, Gaijin-san," she turned and said to my host, "may I bring you something? A drink perhaps?"

"Would you like something—anything?" he asked me.

"What are you having?" I asked him.

"I'd really like an iced tea," he said. "Is that okay? We have soda, juice, all kinds of things for you. What do you want?"

I said, "I'd *love* an iced tea, too." And immediately, Kazuko clapped her hands twice, as if she were in a restaurant, and spoke loudly, "Bobby-san, iced tea for three in the living room—Okay?"

And from some deep recess of the house I heard a distant, "Okay, be right there."

"I take it you have graciously consented to join us," my friend said, bowing lightly to Kazuko.

"Only to pour your drinks and make sure you do not fill the young man's mind with too much silliness." she replied, returning his small bow.

"I told you about her," he smiled at me.

We talked a little, the three of us. I noted she had called him "Gaijin," and asked her why. She laughed and said it was a joke between them. He was actually, she said, one of the few Americans she had met in Japan who seemed appreciative and comfortable with Japanese customs. But, she added, it was also her way of keeping him in line.

She was a delightful woman.

The tea arrived, carried on a tray by my host's son, Bobby. A good-looking little guy whom I imagined to be about 10. After he'd introduced himself to me, and me to him, his father asked if he wanted to stay, but the boy said, "No thanks." He was in the middle of a project, he explained, and he'd see us all later. He started to leave the room, then turned and asked me if I was staying for dinner.

His father asked me, "Would you like to?" I said, "Sure." And Bobby said, "Great, see ya later."

Then his father asked, "What's the project, Young Son?"

Bobby took a step back into the room and said, "I'm making a terrarium."

"For school?" his father asked, leaning his head as far back on the couch as possible and looking at the boy upside down.

"Nope," said Bobby, "for Mom."

"Want some help?" his dad asked.

"Sure," Bobby replied, and I could see he was pleased at the prospect. "But I thought you guys were talking business?"

"Nope," replied my host. "Life. Anyhow, I don't remember asking what you thought about what *we* were doing."

"*Daaad!*" the boy responded in mock complaint.

"So, me to you—yes or no?" his father shot back.

"Yes. You. Now. Greatest dad in the whole wide world," Bobby said, as he quickly knocked the pillow his father had thrown at him safely off to one side. He then stooped to pick it up in the same motion and toss it back with a perfunctory "Here!" to his father, who had stood up and started out of the living room. "Put this back where it belongs, like a good father."

"Bright boy. Charming boy," the Greatest Networker said, sounding like Scrooge on Christmas morning from the movie *A Christmas Carol.* "I think we shall let him live with us for another year," he observed as he left the room, and added in classic Schwarzenegger-ese, "*I'll be baaack.*"

"Kazuko-san, take care of my friend, please," he said over his shoulder, scooping Bobby up off the ground and carrying him off down the hall to the sound of the boy's protests and the kind of laughter that can only come from too much tickling.

* * *

I turned and asked Kazuko how she had come to meet the Greatest Networker and to live here with the family.

"I met him in Japan. How long ago?" she asked herself out loud. "Nine, 10 years now, maybe. He was starting up Network Marketing efforts in Japan and I met him at his very first meeting there.

"I was working as a housekeeper in the home of a wealthy businessman and his family. I cooked, cleaned and took care of the children. It was an unusual family for Japan. Very Western in many ways. Both the mother and father worked. They had been educated in the United States. In fact, that's where they met—and where I met both of them."

"Were you all at the same school here?" I asked.

"Yes," she said. "The father was doing graduate work in business—MBA. His wife was in international law, which was unique for a Japanese woman back then. Still is today, I imagine."

"What college?" I asked.

"Yale," she said.

"What were you studying?"

"I was on a cultural exchange program where drama majors were sent back and forth from Yale to Tokyo University," she answered.

"That seems odd to me," I told her. "You went to Yale, then went back to Japan and became a housekeeper?"

Kazuko laughed. "Yes, I'm sure it does. But truly, I am very happy keeping a house and being part of a family. My children are grown, with children of their own now—" I hoped she didn't notice the expression of shock that must have darted over my face at that revelation "—and I am very devoted to this family. I've adopted them."

"Kazuko . . . may I ask, how old you are?" I offered tentatively.

"56," she said. I told her I found that *very* hard to believe. She smiled and thanked me for my "charm—*and* good manners."

We continued to talk—I have no idea for how long. She was one of the easiest people I had ever spoken with—so natural, so effortless to talk to.

She told me about when the Greatest Networker first came to Japan, about that first opportunity meeting, and how very excited she had been at the prospect of working with him.

She'd learned about Network Marketing while in the United States, she said, and had always thought it was a perfect business for Japanese people. Other companies had come to Japan from America before, but most of them hadn't made the kinds of changes and adjustments in the products—how they were positioned, packaged and presented—or in the business opportunity, that would reflect the unique needs and wants of the Japanese. But his company was different—he had done his homework.

She told me that this first meeting had lasted for six hours! The formal presentation had lasted only about an hour and a half, but everyone had stayed for hours, asking questions about Network Marketing, about how it was done in America, and about how the Greatest Networker thought it could best be done in Japan.

Kazuko told me that the meeting had turned into a seminar on Network Marketing, that my new friend had simply answered every question they asked, and that he had showed and told them all of his ideas about how the business worked best. There were a number of people there who were already involved with other Networking companies, and he'd helped them, too, showing them new ways to offer their products and build their businesses.

"People were amazed," she said. "They had never met someone who was so knowledgeable *and* so willing to share his secrets. A few people with other companies asked if they could sign up with him, but he actually discouraged them! He told them to stay with what they were doing, and offered to help them whenever and however he could.

"It was a remarkable evening," she told me. And then she added, "It certainly changed my life."

"How so?" I asked, thinking of how I felt about . . . was it just this past Thursday? It already seemed weeks ago.

"There were a number of high-powered businessmen present," she replied. "Each one wanted to be 'in charge' of Japan for him. He was very gracious to all of them, but he asked them, please, to wait. He explained that his company's president would arrive the following week, and that *he* would be the one to decide exactly what structure they would use and who would direct what efforts.

"Almost everyone made an appointment to meet with him. I'm sure everybody there wanted to make his pitch to be *ichiban*—the Number One distributor. I stayed until the very end of the meeting and waited until there was no one else left. I went up to him and said, 'Have you scheduled any time to see Japan?' He told me that, in fact, he had set aside the next three days for that very purpose. I asked if he would permit me to be his guide, and he said he'd love that.

"So, the next morning, bright and early, we met at his hotel for breakfast. It was a whirlwind tour." As she spoke, Kazuko actually seemed to re-experience some of the exhilaration as well as the exhaustion of the trip she was describing.

She told me about all the places they visited. How he'd

said he wanted to visit the Peace Park in Hiroshima, how moved he was when they did, and how deeply his emotions had touched her, as well. She described how much he enjoyed the food, from the salty traditional breakfasts and late-night-into-early-morning trips to the *sushi* bars, to a quick bowl of steaming noodles while waiting for the *Shinkansen*—the famous "bullet trains" that rocket across Japan—to the formal 11-course *Kaiseki* diners, which cost more than $500 per person!

Kazuko told me that she'd never been to so many places in her own country in such a short period in her life, and that although it was very rushed, that they both had the most wonderful time.

One high point of the trip for her was a visit to Nara, which Kazuko described as perhaps the most traditional and beautiful of the Japanese cities. She told me that in Nara, you were more likely to see business men and women wearing *kimono* (the classic robe) and *obi* (sash) than anywhere else in modern Japan. They had stayed at the Nara Hotel, in *tatami* rooms with rice-straw floormats and slept on *futons* (Japanese quilts, she explained) which were spread out in layers one on another upon the floor.

As they walked around Nara, which was famous for its Shinto shrines and Buddhist temples and teahouses, they had come upon this one magnificent house enclosed within the most beautiful and peaceful garden she had ever seen.

Kazuko had told him then that this was just the kind of house in which she'd always dreamed of living. She recalled how he had asked if she'd like to buy the house, and how she'd scoffed at his question, saying she could never afford such a beautiful place!

"I've had the same discussion with him about *this* place," I told her.

"Ah, so?" she asked me. "Well, take good care with what you dream, my friend. I have lived in that house in Nara for six years now."

I sat, staring at her for a long time.

Finally, she broke the silence, saying, "Close your mouth now. Flies will go in."

CHAPTER TEN
Appointments with Freedom

I sat, still staring at the Greatest Networker's housekeeper, trying to grasp what she had just told me. She politely ignored my stare, and continued with her recounting of my host's first visit to Japan.

When they finally returned to Tokyo, she said, as they were sitting in his suite at the Imperial Hotel, he'd asked her what would *she* do to establish a Network Marketing business in Japan? Whom would she choose to direct the effort—with whom did she think and feel would she want to work?—by whom would she want to be sponsored?

"It was so much more of a question than I could answer, then" she told me. "I knew that it was terribly important to him, but I honestly felt that any one of the businessmen at the meeting would be a fine choice, and I told him so.

"However, I was concerned that none of them had any

Network Marketing experience, and he said that was really best anyway. That way, he explained, they wouldn't have to *unlearn* the business. It would be difficult enough to help them shed their conventional sales and marketing approaches, without having to change what they thought they knew about Networking, too.

"We talked for a number of hours," she told me, "in fact, well into the next morning. We talked about what I thought would work best in Japan, about how Japanese people worked and lived, and what I thought they valued most and wanted in their lives. I kept trying to get him to tell me what he thought, but he just wanted to know my answers."

"I know exactly what you mean," I told her. "He asks more questions than anyone I've ever met!"

We laughed, and as we did, the Greatest Networker came back into the room and sat down in a chair facing Kazuko and me.

"So," he asked, "did Kazuko enlighten you?"

"She was telling me how you met. How you began your Networking business in Japan. And how you never let *her* ask *you* any questions—which sounded pretty familiar to me," I told him.

He laughed and asked, "Did she tell you she was in charge of our Network in Japan?"

"No," I said with surprise. "She didn't!"

"Kazuko-san," he scolded. "Tell him the truth."

"He chose me to be in charge of our Japanese operations," she said directly. "He caught a lot of flak for that—at first. His company's management wanted a high-powered business man, but he kept telling them to give the job to a *housekeeper*." She

laughed. "Can you imagine how they felt about that? Anyway, he told them I was the best person. I understand they
argued a great deal about it . . . "

"No, we did not," he interrupted. "I simply made them a
deal that was in their best interests."

"Oh, yes—you certainly did *that*." She laughed, turned to
me and said, "He told them to give me the position for one
year, and that if I did not exceed their sales and distributor
goals—by 100 percent!—*he* would sign over *his* commission
checks back to the company *for the next 12 months!*"

"Really?" I was—again—amazed.

"Yes," she said. "What's more, he never told me he'd done
that. I only found out on our first anniversary meeting when
his president and some other company officials from America
came back to Japan."

"Tell the nice man what the sales goal was, Kazuko."

"To reach $500,000 a month in Japan by the end of year
one," she said, matter-of-factly.

"And tell the nice man what you actually accomplished,"
he prodded.

"No, *you* tell him, *Gaijin-san*." She threw it back to him,
pretending displeasure.

"Our little *housekeeper* here," he informed me, "was the
fastest-growing, most successful distributor in the history of
the company—worldwide. Her group, which included all of
Japan, did just under $11 million in total sales for their first
year. Kazuko became a millionaire before the end of her second year in the business."

"*Incredible!*" I gasped, and I must have looked very shocked
indeed, because he pointed to my face and they both burst

out laughing.

"My friend," he said leaning forward toward me, "in this business, you will only achieve what your habits of belief allow. I chose Kazuko because I saw that she believed *anything* was possible. She *had* no limitations in her paradigm for Network Marketing in Japan. She had none for herself, either. She did not *believe* that it couldn't be done—and she refused to listen to anyone who told her otherwise."

"Ignorance is bliss," Kazuko added, smiling. "It's true. I had been blessed with parents who raised me to believe I could do anything I wanted, anything I set my heart and mind to. And that was quite something for a Japanese woman to grow up with, believe me.

"Besides," she said, "my dear friend here spent literally every waking hour of every day with me for almost six months to get our business started. All I did was follow him around, translate and do what he taught me.

"That in itself was one of the most powerful lessons I learned. And I've now done that with all my key people," she added.

"How many leaders do you have?" I asked her.

"Nine key leaders," she told me.

"How many people have you sponsored, totally?" I asked in surprise.

"Oh, 50 or so," she said.

"In 10 years?" I asked—again, quite surprised by her answer.

"Yes," she responded, "in 10 years. That's another thing my *Sensei* here taught me.

"He told me that every highly successful Network Marketer

he had ever met had earned the majority of his or her income from the sales generated by two to five individual distributor groups built by leadership distributors. He said to look for *those* four or five people—to ask all my new people right up front if they were committed to achieving that level of leadership and success, and he told me to focus my efforts on developing those men and women who had made that commitment. So I did."

"What about people who didn't want to make that kind of commitment?" I asked her.

"I gave people what they wanted," she said. "Remember, I'm a housekeeper. I take care of people. So, I simply provided people the level of support and gave them the time and attention that was appropriate for where they were and what they wanted to accomplish. But I was very clear about what *I* wanted. I wanted leaders who would duplicate themselves.

"I never made judgments about what prospects or new distributors wanted," Kazuko said. "I asked *them*. And some of them didn't want to build large Network organizations at first. I knew that for a number of those people, they simply didn't believe great success was possible for them. So, I always worked on establishing habits of belief that supported them in becoming all they truly wanted to achieve. A number of my leaders today were people who had no idea they were capable of such things when they began."

"Do you still sponsor people?" I asked.

"Oh yes," she answered, "but not very often and not usually directly. I help my people downline sponsor, and when I meet someone new and exciting, I match them up with one of my people with whom they'll enjoy working the most."

Well, I sat back even deeper into the couch. I'd heard all of this before. Read it in books and interviews in Networking publications. But I'd never sat face-to-face with someone who'd *actually done it.*

My habits of belief were getting a real stretching lesson here.

"Kazuko," I asked, "I'm sure you're able to retire by now. Why do you keep working your Network Marketing business— and *why* do you still . . . are you still, a *housekeeper?*"

"I am involved in Network Marketing because I love it," she said. "There is nothing else I would rather do. It is how I earn *my living,*" and the emphasis with which she said *my living* made it very clear to me that she meant more than a job or even a career.

"I'm still a *housekeeper,*" she smiled as she said the word, "because I like it. And you know, I've come to realize that housekeeping is excellent training for leadership in Network Marketing. *Really,*" she added, in response to the disbelief on my face.

"Network Marketing is all about taking care of people, and I like taking care of people. Especially this Gaijin-San," she added, pointing bluntly towards my host with one thumb as if she were hitch-hiking. Her obvious affection for my host showed easily through her feigned nonchalance. "This is my *Sensei*—my mentor. It is an honor for me to be with him. I learn constantly from him—and from the family. You haven't met Rachel, yet. You will—he will, yes?" she asked him.

"I trust so," he answered, "though I'm not sure where she is. Have you seen her today, Kaz?"

"No, I haven't," Kazuko replied. "Today's the 25th. Is this

a show day?"

"Every day's a horse show day—in the Spring," he said. "I thought today was clear. I'll have to check my Commitment Book. I know we have an appointment for dinner," he added.

"Commitment Book?" I asked.

"Like an appointment book," he answered.

"You make appointments *with your family?*" The idea of *that* fascinated me.

"Yup," he answered, "with Rachel and the kids, too."

"Ah . . . " I asked hesitatingly, "would you tell me about that?"

"Sure. What do you want to know?" he asked.

"Well, it seems strange to make appointments with your own family," I said.

"That's a nice opinion," he said. Then he repeated, "So, what did you want to know?"

"Well, ah . . . it seems a little cold—doesn't it?"

"Not to me," he answered. "It works for us. I make business appointments and I make family appointments. Making them helps me keep them. They're my commitments."

"But," I said, "doesn't that take the spontaneity out of things?"

"Just the opposite," he said. "That's one way I make certain I have the time for being spontaneous." He noted my puzzled look. "Let me explain.

"There was a time when my family took second place to my work. Truth is, far-distant second. I love working. There's nothing in this world I'd rather do. And because of that, I was putting my family second. I'd get to them when it was convenient—when there was 'free time' after my business was completed.

"Well, at one point I noticed there never was any 'free time.' Every time some space would show up, so would something to fill it. I had my life all scheduled and no time for them—and no time for myself, for that matter.

"So I asked, what's missing? What did I need to do to make the time I wanted to be with my family, and to do the things I wanted to do for myself, as well?

"Two things were missing," he said, "and the first was simple: making a commitment and keeping it. I knew I could do that. I was making business commitments—and keeping darn near every one of those. It seemed a simple matter to me—not necessarily easy, but simple. If I could do that with my business, there was no reason I couldn't do it with every other area of my life.

"So, I started making appointments for specific times to be with Rachel and the kids. I told them what I was doing and why, and they agreed to help me keep the appointments I made with them, because we all saw them as commitments now—not just appointments.

"I made dates with Rachel—dinner dates, dates to watch videos after the kids went to sleep, we even scheduled a couple of weekend seminars at local hotels. I'll let you figure out what the subject matter was.

"Rachel and I scheduled 30 minutes every day at 9:00 in the morning to talk with each other about what was happening in our work and lives. When either of us was traveling, we did that over the phone.

"I made appointments with Bobby, too. I hired him as my 'Fun Coach,' because I saw that fun was missing as well—you know, 'All work and no play . . . ' Bobby'd take me out and play ball—which is how I became a tee-ball coach, by the way. We'd go for walks, have adventures. I just let him be the coach and show me what to do.

"Rebecca was a bit more difficult at first. Her only sugges-tion—outside of horses—was to have me go shopping with her. Dad as wallet. I'd already mastered that one, so we stuck with horses.

"I hadn't ridden in, gee . . . " he closed his eyes, thinking, " . . . in almost 20 years. And then only in a Western saddle. She taught me English-style riding. She taught me to jump, too. It's great. She's a wonderful teacher, and now, I have two lessons a week with her. Dad as student, client *and* paying customer.

"The question of 'cold' or 'spontaneous' never occurs to me. What's important is, does this way of doing things em-power me and empower my family? It has—for years. So, I conclude—it works. It may not work for you."

"No," I protested, "I understand. It really sounds like a great way to make sure you balance those two areas of your life. I want to try it.

"You know," I added, "keeping a commitment book like that, and including appointments with your family, is kind of like creating a habit of belief, isn't it?"

"Bright boy. Charming boy," the Greatest Networker said, just as he had done earlier with Bobby, and sounding again like the transformed Scrooge.

"Can we finish our talk about habits?" I asked.

"Let's!" he said, leaning forward and rubbed his hands quickly back and forth with a smile. "But first—remember, I said there were two things I found which were missing in my being able to spend time in my life where I really wanted."

"Yes, you did," I agreed. "Making and keeping your commitments was one. What's the other?"

"As soon as I began to honor my commitments, what showed up immediately was how little freedom I had with my job to make new ones." He spoke slowly and with emphasis, as if treating a very serious topic. Which, I immediately realized, he was. "I thought I was a big deal. You know, six-figure salary, all the benefits, called the shots. After all, I owned my own business and I was the boss. WRONG!

"To tell the truth, I was shocked when I saw how little freedom I actually had." He stood straight up and spread out his arms, as if drawing a weighty conclusion for a college seminar. "*Time* was what was missing most! And I knew, the only way to have more of it was to *create my life—and my work—with more time to do what I wanted.*"

"And that's where Network Marketing entered the picture?" I guessed.

"And that's where Network Marketing entered the picture." He nodded in assent. "I'd known about Network Marketing for years. I thought it was interesting, possibly even very powerful, but I didn't really understand it. I had too much baggage from being a conventional marketing man to see what the possibilities were. You could say—and you'd be right—that my habits of belief didn't permit me to see myself being successful in Network Marketing."

"So, what did you do?" I asked, fascinated.

"Well, I knew I'd have to unlearn lots—and I knew that would be hard for me. I can be pretty stubborn."

"I'll say," Kazuko chimed in.

He made a face at her and continued, letting out a deep breath as he spoke. "So, I selected a company with a superb reputation—one which had been around long enough for the unique ups and downs of this business to make them strong, which had solid management with field experience, an excellent product line consumers loved once they tried and would continue to use forever, so there was residual income involved—and, the very best sponsor I could find.

"In fact, the sponsor I wanted," he continued dramatically, "was the Greatest Networker in the World."

"Whoa!" I exclaimed. "Wait just a minute. I thought *you* were the Greatest Networker in the World!"

"Yes, some people say that," he admitted. "But if that's true, what does that make the person who taught *me* everything I know about this business?"

"I see . . . " I said unconvincingly. I didn't. This Hitchcockian twist had my mind spinning more than a little. I sat there stunned. There's an even greater Networker than he is? I looked over at him, and then at Kazuko, and they just sat there grinning, like two kids just barely keeping a secret. No answers there.

"Okay . . ." I said, expecting to say more, but nothing came to mind or mouth.

"Come on," he said, standing up and rescuing me. "Let's go find my sponsor."

It's her! I thought. It's got to be his wife, Rachel. "This is amazing!" I announced to myself out loud, as I followed him and Kazuko out of the room and out of the house.

CHAPTER ELEVEN

Habits of Disbelief

W e walked across the flagstone parking area in front of the house, past his office-study and on down to the horse barn. As we approached the stables, I saw a long horse trailer—the kind that would hold at least four horses attached to a hefty-looking pickup truck with an extra set of back wheels.

There was a clomping of hooves and the sound of voices coming from within the trailer as we walked along its side to the end where a young woman was coaxing a tall grey mare backwards down the loading ramp. The entire length of the horse's neck and upraised head towered high above her.

"Oh, come on," she chided the horse. "You know what to do. Stop being so stubborn . . . " the girl said, as the horse came off the ramp and wheeled around prancing and moving sideways.

" . . . Unlike her owner?" my host commented. "How'd you do, Becc?" he asked the girl whom I assumed was his daughter

Rebecca.

"I was awful!" she said emphatically, "but Mom was brilliant! Four blues—and one *green!*"

"*Sixth!* What happened?" he asked.

"My saddle squeaked!" came the answer from within the trailer.

"She lost it, too—with the judge," Rebecca said with a laugh. "You should have seen her, Dad. She was livid. I thought she was going to punch him in the nose. She told him next time she'd oil her butt, and stomped off.

"What's really funny," she continued, "is he's the judge she's hired for the Red Mountain Show!"

"Young lady . . . !" admonished the voice emerging from the trailer, " . . . forget it! Oh, I was so . . . Ugh! That *man*" . . . and the angry voice trailed off.

Standing before me—clad in the high black boots, riding britches, tailored blue blazer and white blouse with the high collar of an equestrian—was Rachel. She pulled a net off her hair and shook her head rapidly back and forth, her thick, long chestnut hair spreading out around her head, making her look like a most attractive version of Medusa.

She looked over at me. Walked over to me. Stuck out her hand, and in the softest, deepest, most alluring voice, said, "I'm Rachel, and I am the nicest, most demure woman you will ever meet . . . " then abruptly changed her voice to loud and strong to the point of venomous, " . . . and I am so *ticked off that I am not fit to be pleasant to you or any other mortal! Forgive me!*" she declared dramatically, and stomped off into the barn.

I stood there in shocked silence. So did everyone else.

Slowly the silence was replaced with the kind of giggles and snickers that emerge after laughter's been held in as long as humanly possible. Everyone burst out laughing, my host most of all.

All I could manage was a smile. I felt I dared not join in.

Finally, as everyone composed themselves, Kazuko said, "I go to make ready the queen's bath. Should I up the temperature 20° or so?"

"Don't bother," said my host. "The minute she gets in it will shoot up higher than that! Boy, is she steamed. I don't think I've seen her so angry at anyone besides me—and *that* was at least 12 years ago, and I was still drinking! Whew! Rebecca—did she actually *hit* him?"

"*No, Daad,*" said the girl, "but she should have. It was really uncalled for. She had a perfect ride—and Cassi was perfect, too. I think he just didn't want her to take *all* her classes."

"Looks like he picked the wrong lady to be overly fair with today," he observed. "How did she find out about the squeaking bit? Did she see the sheet?"

"Yeah," Rebecca said. "She made a beeline for the judge's stand after the class. We all told her not to go up, but there was no stopping her. Dad, she had smoke pouring out of her ears."

"I'll bet," he laughed. "Well," he said as he turned to me, "you've just seen the most powerful woman I know, being . . . well . . . *powerful.* Ah me. She's something, she is.

"*You're beautiful when you're furious,*" he shouted in the direction of the barn, as he grabbed Rebecca and me by our arms and started toward the house, whispering, "Let's get out of here."

We'd been in the living room talking for about 40 minutes—Rebecca had joined us after her shower—when Rachel came in.

As she said she would, Kazuko had made the bath ready for her, adding candlelight and incense to sooth her, Kaz told us. She had laid out Rachel's favorite robe and a glass of lemonade—which Rachel now placed on the coffee table as she sat down next to me on the couch.

She put her arm through mine and looked directly into my eyes and said, "Well, you must be pretty special. I haven't delivered a performance like *that* in at least seven years,"—I heard the Networker chuckle—"and even then I reserved my *melodrama* only for my husband. So, what makes you so special?" she asked.

Before I could say a word, she spoke quickly, "Oh, he's blushing," and she squeezed my arm with hers. "I like him," she informed her husband, and she smiled over at me. "Where'd he come from?" she asked no one in particular.

"I met him Thursday evening at the meeting in town," said my host. "I asked him to come to visit Friday, and we've been together ever since."

"So," Rachel turned back to me, "what have you been doing?"

"I really don't know where to begin — there's been so much . . . " I was coming close to stammering again.

"Relax," she said patting my arm. "This isn't a quiz." She laughed and leaned forward to sip her drink.

"So, madame," Kazuko spoke. "You've had quite a day—yes?"

"Yes," Rachel said, "and thank you, Kaz, for the wonderful

bath, the candles, the lemonade. You're a dear."

"Pleasure," Kazuko replied. "You looked like you needed it."

"*Fer sure,*" Rachel replied in a perfectly-pitched Valley Girl voice. She turned to me again and asked, "So, really, what have you guys been doing and talking about since you got here?"

I tried my best to report on all the things we had said and done. As I did, I realized what a massive amount of information, thought, new ideas and experiences I been exposed to—all in less than 24 hours!

By now, I'm sure you expect me to say "Amazing"—so I won't disappoint you. That's precisely what it was for me. *Amazing.*

"Well," declared Rachel, when I'd finished cataloging all I had seen, heard and done, "seems we've all had a pretty full day. Tell me," she asked me, "what's next for you?"

"The place to start," I began, "is to form habits of belief which support my goals."

"Bright boy—Charming boy," she said to her husband.

"I've told him so," he agreed. "Quick study, too."

"Good," Rachel said, and turning back to me, asked, "So, where will you begin?"

"Ah," I pondered out loud, "with my goals—and some general habits of belief I already know will support whatever I decide to achieve."

"Want a suggestion?" she asked.

"Sure," I said.

"Play with your belief habits first."

"Tell me why you say that?" I asked.

[99]

"No," she said flatly, though gently. "You tell me."

I was beginning to see what a powerful pair these two were—and, where the Greatest Networker got some of his Greatest Networker-ness.

"Okay," I said, slowly. "I suspect that my habits of *disbelief* . . ." and I paused for their reaction to my use of that phrase. It came instantly.

"Good!" he said. Rachel smiled and said, "Continue, my clever friend."

I did.

" . . . My habits of *disbelief* affect my ability to create my goals realistically—and by that I mean without the limitations of what I've *thought* was possible. The kinds of habits I have now—or at least, *have had, until now*—have gotten me to where I am now. So, they obviously need some work, because I'm not where I want to be.

"So," I continued, "first step—balance, or *begin* to balance my scales.

"Bright boy—Charming boy?" I asked them.

"Touché," said Rachel. "And true, too."

"Okay," said the *Second* Greatest Networker, leaning forward from his seat, "and how is that done?"

"That's *my* question for you—both," I said, and I sat back, waiting to see what came next.

CHAPTER TWELVE
Pictures of Belief

M y instruction continued with a slight change of venue. We'd all moved from the living room to the kitchen.

Time, again, was flying and it was past six o'clock when Kazuko inquired if anyone was interested in eating. A unanimous "Yes" sent Rebecca off to look for Bobby, and Rachel to change her clothes, while the rest of us went in to prepare dinner.

The kitchen was on a grand scale like the rest of house. Big to the point of huge—more like the kitchen of a restaurant— and many of the appliances were the commercial kind, like the big charcoal gray, eight-burner gas stove and the gleaming, stainless steel refrigerator which looked to be at least two or three times the size one would normally find in a private home.

Still in all, this room, too, held a genuine warmth. Clearly, this was *the* center of their home. I could tell that more living was done here in the kitchen than in the living room, or in any other part of the house, for that matter.

Everyone took part in the preparations. I was enrolled in slicing vegetables, expertly directed by Rebecca, who explained in great detail how carrots were best cut on a diagonal to provide them with the fullest spectrum of both flavor and "essential energy."

"Yin and yang," Kazuko interjected into my lesson. "This way, we get the most from the carrot, because this way of cutting it provides the greatest balance of the vegetable's natural life force."

"Heaven and earth—together," Rebecca interjected.

"So now I'm *really* going to get a taste of philosophy?" I mused out loud, and they all laughed with me.

We were all working around an island in the center of the kitchen. Its top was a giant slab of dark butcher's block strips of what I learned was teak wood. At one end was a double sink where all the vegetables and fish (shrimp, clams, some kind of thin filets of a pale, almost translucent fish, scallops, and . . . yes, it was . . . *lobster!*) that were being used for dinner, were all washed thoroughly.

Above the island were a tremendous variety of shapes and sizes and colors of pots and pans hanging from a strong, wrought-iron affair which was suspended from the high, arched ceiling. And the whole contraption was covered in tiny white twinkle lights. It was always Christmas in this kitchen.

Our completed preparations for dinner amounted to four big platters. Three were covered with assorted, sliced vegetables: carrots, squash, Chinese cabbage, leeks, scallions, broccoli, green and red bell peppers, pea pods, and tiny, miniature ears of corn. The other was a sumptuous array of fish and sea-food. And each platter was arranged as if it were going to be photographed for a magazine like *Food & Wine*.

We all stood there gazing at this marvelous array until I could no longer contain myself, and asked, "Now what?"

"Nabe!" exclaimed Bobby. (He pronounced it Nah-Bay, with a strong and long "a.")

"What's a nabe?" I asked.

Rachel described what's called the traditional "One Pot" cooking of Japan, where everything is cooked right in front of you at the dinner table in *one . . . pot . . . .* The assembled diners sit around this boiling pot of clear soup, heated from beneath by a portable gas burner, she told me, and select what they want to eat from the platters of vegetables, fish and shellfish, put it in the pot and take it back out when it's cooked. There are usually bowls of rice and a series of sauces in which to dip the food, too.

Kazuko explained that in Japan, nabe was a dish eaten mostly in the winter and fall. But, she told me, since the members of *this* family were only "country samurai," it was permissible to have nabe any time.

We ate at a wonderful old wooden table tucked comfortably into an alcove in the L-shaped kitchen. As we selected, dipped and retrieved our food (all done, by the way, with wooden chopsticks) Rachel asked me, "So, we were talking about your habits of belief . . . needing to balance the scales with new habits . . . and you were about to ask us how that was done—right?"

"Yes," I said.

"Well," Rachel replied, "I'd like to hear what you would

do, first."

"Okay," I said, by now not at all surprised that the issue had been promptly dropped back in my lap. "I'd go back to the movie of my life that your husband did with me. Do you know the exercise?" I asked her.

"She does," my host spoke up. "She taught it to me."

"Oh," I laughed. "I see."

"So," I continued, "I'd take some of the scenes from that movie and build beliefs, new, positive habits of belief around them."

"Great," said Rachel. "Tell me about a couple . . . tell me one habit of belief you have now, and what new one you'd replace it with from your movie."

"Well," I thought out loud, "I believe that I cannot speak in front of a group. I mean, I can, obviously, but I don't like to. I'm not very good at it. But in my movie, I was up on stage and I had the audience responding to me just like I was a first-class speaker."

"Good," Rachel said. "Describe what that's like. Give me the details. What's it like for you being a first-class speaker?"

I did my best to comply with Rachel's request. I was hesitant at first. It was awkward, because it seemed like . . . well . . . a lie. She noticed my difficulty and asked me what was going on and I told her how foolish it all sounded.

"I understand," she said. "It's probably going to be like that at first. Just know that because of all the old habits you've formed over the years, these new ideas and images may seem silly to you now. After all, you *know* you're not a polished speaker, so the very idea of saying or believing you are something you are not seems ridiculous."

"But I can see," I interrupted, "that it's the way to go. I mean, I know what's going on here is, I've got one old habit rejecting a new one. It's kinda like the old habit is fighting for its life a bit."

"*Very good!*" Rachel said, and I could see she was genuinely pleased.

"Charming boy," her husband added.

"Go on, go on," she encouraged.

"Well," I said—and sighed deeply, closing my eyes to bring to mind the image of me standing on the stage in front of that applauding crowd.

I was shaken out of my imagination by Rachel's hand on my arm and her gentle, yet insistent, "What were you doing just now?"

"Well," I told her, "I was bringing up the picture of that scene from my movie and looking at it . . . remembering what it was like. What they looked like. How I felt. The sound of their applause."

"Terrific!" she exclaimed.

"Why so terrific?" I inquired.

"Because *that*, what you just did, remembering that picture in your mind, is exactly the process you use to alter any habit of belief you have on any subject, anywhere, anytime.

"Even though these pictures are imagined, your mind accepts them as if they were real, as if they were actual experiences you've had and were simply remembering.

"See," she continued, "you're balancing the scales, adding new images, new pictures of your new beliefs. Your mind works in geometric progression, too. It just keeps multiplying the number of times you 'remember' or relive the experience. In no time the scales will begin to swing the other way.

"In fact, they have already. Once they start to pick up some momentum—even just a little—swinging in a new and opposite, positive direction, you'll change your actions in direct proportion to your changing scales—to your changing habits of belief. Do you see what I'm saying?"

"*See what I'm saying . . . ?*" Odd, I actually did *see* what Rachel was *saying*. I had in my mind this picture of this set of scales with a pile of stuff weighting down one side, shifting and beginning to have the other side grow heavier—even begin to take on a kind of glow of importance as it sank down. I told her what I saw.

Rachel sat back in her chair and looked at me with a broad smile, "I could look at you—or, hug you," she said. "I think I'll look first."

"What does the other side look like?" the Greatest Networker asked me.

"Excuse me?" I said, not understanding what he meant.

"The other side of the scales," he said. "You told us the side that was getting heavier was . . . what did you say? Glowing? What did the other side that was moving up look like?"

I closed my eyes and imagined the scales. I described for him what I saw.

I saw them moving—the scales. One side becoming heavier, glowing with a kind of . . . well . . . sparkle, almost. The other side was much darker, yet these somber-colored shapes were kind of . . . floating.

This was wild! I never did stuff like this. I never see pictures like this in my mind. It was like watching television—or a movie.

"What do you make of that?" he asked me.

"Gosh," I said, feeling—and speaking—like my habitual teenager voice. "It's like the old beliefs are getting lighter and just floating away."

"*Fantastic!*" he exclaimed.

"What does it mean?" I asked.

"No idea," he replied. "Sounds great though—doesn't it?"

I admitted it did—and felt great, too. I actually felt physically lighter. My normal background of worry and preoccupation with the future of things was gone. In their place, I felt . . . *confident.*

"It's nice to have you show up," Rachel remarked.

I must have looked puzzled, because she arched her eyebrows and opened her eyes wide, and explained, "It's nice to have you be here. Right here. I noticed that sometimes before you seemed to be somewhere else. Kind of *there*, not *here*."

"Out to lunch," I said and laughed.

They both laughed with me, nodding their heads in a "yes" direction.

We sat in silence for a time. My mind was flooded with images from my movie, doing things I've always wanted, acting with people in ways I've dreamed of being. I didn't even close my eyes. The pictures just flashed freely into and out of my mind.

At last I said, "This is it—isn't it? This is how you form new habits—mental habits of belief that support you in creating what you want in your life. Amazing."

"Yes, it is," Rachel said.

"Mom," Rebecca spoke up, "tell him about your day planner,

your commitment book."

"What about it?" I asked, turning to Rachel.

"You know what a day planner is?" she asked.

"A daily calendar book where you keep appointments and stuff—like the commitment book your husband told me about?" I asked in return.

"Yes," she said, "exactly. Becca and I each have a clear plastic insert in our day planners—same typed page slipped inside, both sides, so you can read it whether it's facing left or right—with a complete description of all the habits of belief we want to create on them.

"We read them every day, first thing—and every night, just before we go to bed. Throughout the day, whenever I glance at my commitments and things to be done, I pick out a sentence or a whole paragraph, read it, then close my eyes and imagine the picture of me doing that or being that. I guess I probably do that 20 or 30 times every day. I've done it for years now."

"That's how I got my horses," Rebecca told me. "I put a couple of pages in my three-ring binder notebook at school. One was the story I wrote about me having my horses. The other was a whole bunch of pictures cut out from magazines and books." She added confidentially, "I thought Dad was going to shoot me when he found the horse books I used from the library with the pictures cut out."

"I did shoot you," he replied. "I have a picture of me doing so in *my* commitment book!"

And we all laughed.

"Seriously," Rebecca said. "I looked at it every day. Lots of times. One day," she said covering her impish smile temporarily with her hand, "I was looking at it in English class, when the teacher snuck up behind me and asked what I was doing. I was really embarrassed. But, I told her the truth—what it was, and what I was doing it for, and I guess she thought it was okay . . . "

"Okay?!" her father interrupted. "I'll say," he said as he reached across the table and messed up the hair on top of her head—all to Rebecca's protests of "*Daaad.*"

"The teacher made the whole thing into an assignment," he said, with obvious pride and delight. "She had Becc's entire class construct their own stories of beliefs they wanted, bring in magazines—*not books!*" he said glaring at Rebecca. ". . . cut out pictures and paste them on the back side of the stories they'd written. She even made a requirement that they all include in their stories *and* pictures getting an A in English that term. No kidding."

"Did they?" I asked Rebecca.

"Yes," she replied, shyly looking down for a moment.

"*The whole class—everyone?*" I asked in disbelief.

"The whole class," Rebecca replied, and this time, all shyness was gone from her face and voice.

I was sold.

"Anyway," Rebecca continued, "I got my own horse about, oh, six months after I started changing my beliefs."

"Wrong," her father said.

"*Wrong*—that's right," Rebecca added. "Two horses."

"*Oh, come on,*" I said, astonished.

"True," Rachel told me. "We'd told Rebecca we would support her having a horse of her own, and she'd have to get the horse herself. So, she worked after school mucking stalls and helping at a farm that friends of ours have down the road.

"They had a lovely, grey thoroughbred mare and her filly that didn't get along with any of their other horses. They would kick and bite whenever they were with other horses, and nobody liked riding them. They'd had them for sale for months, but no one wanted to buy them. Rachel seemed to be the only one who could control the mare, and one day they just up and gave Rebecca both horses."

"*Unbelievable*," I said, leaning back on the legs of my chair.

I came forward with a thunk, turned to Bobby and asked, "And what strange and wonderful tales of great accomplishments do you have to tell me?"

"First place at the science fair . . . Tee-ball Season and Tournament Champs . . . My bike . . ."

"Stop. *Stop!*" I exclaimed. "I get the message."

"Would you like to hear about how I got my house?" Kazuko asked.

"Don't try to stop *her*," the Greatest Networker advised.

"I walked up to the house with my camera one day on a Networking visit back to Nara," Kazuko told me. "I politely explained to the people who answered the door that it was the most beautiful house and garden I had ever seen. I asked permission to take a picture of it, and after hearing that I wanted one just like it and why I wanted the pictures—how I was going to use them to create habits of belief for having such a house—the owners were intrigued. They suggested *they* take pictures of me on the walk, in the garden, in the living room. They showed me the whole house, explained its history, invited me for dinner, too.

"I signed them up that night in Network Marketing," she

laughed. "They are two of my leaders. Dear friends, now. And, about two years after we met, they wanted to move to be with their children in Yokohama and asked me please to purchase their house. It was important to them, they said, that the person who owned it loved it as they did and would preserve its history and beauty. So, I bought it."

"Lesson Number Seventy-Four, complete?" my host asked, putting his hand on my shoulder.

"Complete," I replied.

"Good," he said standing up from his chair. "Guys' night for dishes. Ladies—split," he commanded.

"He always does the dishes when there's only one pot to clean," Rebecca observed wryly as she left the kitchen skipping through the door.

"He's a bright and charming man," added Rachel.

Kazuko bowed, smiled and left us to our work.

CHAPTER THIRTEEN
Teaching Teachers

A s we were leaving the kitchen, the Greatest Networker turned to me and asked, did I play billiards? "Pool?" I asked in return.

"No, billiards," he replied. "No pockets. Three balls. Two white—one red."

I said I'd never played, though I'd seen tables like that before and had wondered about the game.

He took me through another part of the house, off to the opposite side of the living room, to a wonderful room that seemed right out of a gentleman's club in Britain or Philadelphia. I fully expected a couple of old, white-bearded gents in smoking jackets, holding cigars and brandy snifters, to show up at any moment.

The room was arranged around a vividly green billiard table, made all the more bright by a bank of three sets of shaded lights clustered together that hung in a straight row down from the ceiling above the table lengthwise. The table itself was an antique—heavy and old, with ornate hand carvings all over the sides and claw-and-ball feet. There was a brass plaque on one end which read, "Presented to Anthony and Rebecca. Happy 30th Anniversary."

I looked up at him after reading the inscription and he answered my unspoken question.

"Rachel's mother and father. Her dad taught her to play, she taught me. She is, as you've seen, a superb teacher," he said.

"She is that," I agreed.

"What makes her so good . . . " he said, handing me a cue after rolling it back and forth on the table two or three times, with a "Try this one," " . . . is her devotion to having her students surpass her. No matter what subject she's teaching—riding, billiards, Network Marketing—she is absolutely intent on having you go further than she's gone.

"Remarkable woman," he added with love, respect and obvious pride.

He briefly explained the object of the game to me: we each had one of the two white "cue" balls as our own for the duration of the game, and the task was to hit each of the other two "object" balls with our own cue ball to score a point. He proceeded to show me how it was done by running 38 points before finally missing what he explained was "an easy, three-cushion shot."

Remarkably, I made six shots in a row before sitting down for his turn.

As we took our shots and between my asking his advice on where to aim or what kind of "English"—or spin—to put on the ball, we talked about all kinds of things.

The room had a series of hunting prints and stuffed animals around on the walls. He said he wasn't a hunter, although he loved guns and shooting. He stuck to killing clay pigeons, rather than real ones, he said, adding, "Though Kazuko had never figured out how to cook them very well."

The animals were Rachel's father's. He was a sportsman and my host had kept his trophies more for the memory of him than anything else.

I asked him what Rachel's father was like.

"He taught me to shoot," he replied, ". . . and more—much, much more.

"He considered it a flaw in my character that I didn't enjoy hunting *real* animals. He was a pretty macho guy—a Teddy Roosevelt type. He used to tell me that he only bothered keeping *my* company because Rachel was so fond of me. He was a most remarkable man.

"Tony was successful in business," he continued. "Not rich, but he worked hard and did very well for himself and his family. Rachel was their only child, and Tony always considered her his oldest son—the heir to his family name. I fully expected him to insist I take his name when Rachel and I got married.

"When Rachel was nearly 16, she wanted a car—a red Corvette. Tony said, 'Okay, I'll get you one. But how can I be sure you'll value it and take proper care of it?' She didn't know the answer to that, so he told her he'd think of a way *for her.* And he certainly did *that.*

"On her 16th birthday, he gives her this small gift-wrapped box and inside is the key to a new Corvette—and a phone number on a piece of paper. I can just see her, jumping up and down all excited, throwing her arms around him—you know?"

I nodded.

He continued.

"So Rachel asks, 'Where is it? Where's my car?' And he tells her it's in the garage. So she runs to the garage to see it, and there it is—*in pieces!*"

I must have looked shocked, because he said, "No kidding—*in pieces—hundreds of them!* He'd bought her the car all right, and then he had a local mechanic take it completely apart—engine and everything—and lay it all out all over the garage floor!"

"Amazing," I said. And it was. I told him I couldn't imagine someone doing that!

"Boy, I couldn't either," he said. "Until I met Tony, that is.

"So, picture this, there's Rachel, she's standing there looking at all these parts scattered all over the place and he comes up to her and asks, 'Don't you want to know what the phone number's for?' She says, yes, and he tells her that's the name of the mechanic who'll help her put the car back together again. He's expecting her call, he says."

"What did Rachel do?" I asked, still incredulous at the whole affair.

"She put it together," he said matter-of-factly. "Took her four months of nights and weekends, but she did it. She drove that car for over 17 years. He was right. She took incredible care of it."

"That's amazing," I said.

"Tony was amazing," he said, shaking his head with the memory of the man.

From his use of the word "was," I assumed that his father-in-law was no longer living, so I didn't ask about that.

He asked if I'd like to see the guns Tony had given him. I'd never owned a gun—not even a toy as a child. My mother was adamant about "No guns!" But, I do admire craftsmanship and quality—of any kind—and the guns he showed me were magical. You could see and feel how fine they were. They had the spirit of excellence about them.

His pride and joy were a magnificent pair of matched Weatherby "his and hers" field shotguns, fitted into a wooden, green velvet-lined case that had belonged to his father-in-law. 12 gauge for him; the lighter 20 gauge was a woman's gun. Much of the metalwork on the guns was engraved in hunting scenes like the prints that were hanging on the walls.

I asked if he and Rachel shot together and he said they had. I asked who was the better shot and he said he was. I asked if he intended to teach Rachel to be better than he was—and he said, "No."

"I've already got enough trouble keeping up with her. Besides, if Tony didn't teach her to be a crack shot, you can be sure she wasn't all that interested. So, I'll get to keep being a better shot for myself—at least, for a little while longer," he laughed and then promptly missed a truly easy billiard shot. "Whoops," he said, "I think Tony's trying to tell me something."

We played and talked for another hour or so. I did well, especially for the first time playing the game. He showed me how to make the basic shots, the break shot, and how to use different kinds of English for different situations.

I thoroughly enjoyed the game.

"Billiards is very much like Network Marketing," he told me. "In many ways.

"It's a game of position. Certainly the shot right in front of you is important, but you must also think ahead two, three shots or more. You want to make the first one successfully, but you're always planning for the next one . . . where the balls will end up after you complete that shot. That way, you can easily string together 10, 20, 30 successful points or more."

"Don't you lose your focus when you're planning so far ahead?" I asked.

"No," he said. "You expand your focus, enlarge it to include the future." He stood up, away from the table and leaned on his cue. "You're making sure you see the big picture . . . how one action fits into another and then another. That also builds momentum. And when you approach your business-building from that larger perspective, your priorities shift and you begin to focus on longer-term concerns."

"Such as?" I asked him.

"Teaching teachers is a good example," he told me.

"Usually, when you're concentrating on teaching people to teach people, your results are slower in coming than if you focused on simply teaching people how to sell products and sponsor people. That's a simpler job, and it yields larger results faster in terms of generating sales income—at least at first.

"But when you teach people to teach people, you move from creating results to empowering others.

"Of course, that's a result, too. But it's bigger. What you'll end up with is longer-lasting success, more leaders and more leadership in your organization, which ultimately results in both greater stability and greater productivity.

"Do you remember how I told you I began, with significant success for myself, but no one else was doing the business successfully?"

"Yes," I answered.

"It's like that," he said. "When I came to understand how the business works, that it depends on our ability to effectively sponsor people who know how to teach people how to teach other people, my business began to grow for real. I suppose I could have taught people to write compelling sales letters, but that's not what drives this business—and it certainly wasn't what drives me. I've developed a number of persuasive letters people can use to get their prospects to take a look at the opportunity, and my people use them with good success. But after that—what happens? After they've agreed to take a look, what do people do then?"

"Ask questions?" I answered.

"You bet!" he replied, "but about what? See, unless you've been taught to help people discover or reveal their own values and what's really important to them, you can't connect your opportunity to anything lasting or meaningful in their lives. It's not anchored *to them*. You might come across the rare one or two folks who are self-motivated, who already understand Network Marketing, people, sales—the unique way we do it in this business, and how to teach and train others— but they are very rare birds indeed.

"For the most part, you'll be working with inexperienced people, turning them into professionals. And, 'professional whats?' is a good question. Professional teachers."

He paused for a moment, closing his eyes, and I knew he was creating a picture of what he wanted to say. I closed my eyes just for the heck of it to see if I could come up with a picture of what he was going to talk about. When I opened my eyes, he was staring at me.

"Falling asleep on me?" he asked humorously.

I explained what I was doing and he shot out one of his booming laughs that echoed all around the wooden walls and terra cotta tiles of the billiard room.

"Well . . . ?" he asked. "What'd ya get?"

"I remembered this story I heard from a workshop leader back in New England. He was telling a group of us about a music professor he'd had in college. He said he walked in the first day—thinking he was pretty good—and the teacher put a horrendously difficult piece of music on the stand and told him to play it. He slaughtered it. He was *awful!* His teacher sent him home to practice.

"Next week, he showed up for his lesson expecting to play the piece he was given for homework, but instead, the teacher put a new, even harder piece in front of him. He thought he was bad before, *but this one was ridiculous!* He was more than awful.

"This continued for another couple of weeks; he'd murder the piece in class, take it home to practice, come back and be given one twice as difficult as the one he hadn't even come close to mastering from the week before. Finally, he was so upset and frustrated, he exploded all over his teacher. 'Why this . . . ? What . . . ?' And the teacher pulled out the very first piece he'd given him and said sternly, '*Play it.*' And he did—

beautifully!

"He was amazed. The teacher took that one away and put the second lesson on the stand and said, 'Play that.' And he did—he was great! So, he looked at the teacher and the teacher said, 'Robert, if I left you to your own devices, you'd still be practicing that very first lesson—and you *still* wouldn't be able to do it right. I don't care about your playing one piece. I care about your *playing!*'

"That's what I got," I said.

The Greatest Networker just looked at me in silence before he replied—he was visibly excited, and he began to pace about and gesture as he spoke. "That's a fantastic story," he said. *"That's great!* It not only illustrates teaching somebody more than . . . well, like teaching a man to fish instead of giving him a fish. You know, when you teach him to fish you feed him for an entire lifetime, instead of just one meal.

"But it also illustrates the whole business of stretching—going beyond your comfort zone. That student was stretched far beyond where he himself would have ever gone all by himself. Boy, he had a great teacher. I'd like to have that guy in my Networking business!"

"What guy?" asked Rachel entering the room, and to her husband asked, "Ready for our walk?" She was dressed in jeans with chambry, work shirt and a pair of used, canvas Keds. She looked like a college girl.

"Sure, let me change and I'll be right down," he said. He was still dressed in his sarong. I noticed I was, too.

"No need," she said, and tossed him a pair of jeans and sneakers with socks.

"Great," he said. "I'll go get these on. Tell Rachel that story you just told me—then come for a walk with us, okay?"

I looked at Rachel. "He asked you," she said.

I pointed to my sarong.

"Ooops," she said. "Your clothes are still in the bath—yes?"

"Yes," I replied.

"Come on," she said, signaling me to follow her. "Let's get your clothes and you can tell me your story."

"Okay, I agreed," and as my host ducked into the small bathroom off the billiard room I walked with Rachel to get my clothes and told her my story.

She had much the same reaction as he had. "What a great story!" she said.

"Can you say more about teaching teachers?" I asked as we reached the bath. I picked up my clothes and must have looked a little lost—there was no room to change in. Rachel smiled, pointed to the clothes in my hand, and just said, "Please," as she ducked out of the room to wait outside, leaving the door slightly ajar so we could continue speaking.

As I changed, she explained about teaching teachers, speaking loudly so I'd hear her clearly.

"Have you ever seen a Karate master break through boards or bricks?" she called.

"Yes," I said.

"Can you picture where he is concentrating all his energy?"

"Towards the center of the middle board," I reasoned.

"Nope. That sounds logical—but it doesn't work that way. He directs his all energy to a point *just below the last board*. That's where the focus is . . . the goal. In that way, the Karate master assures that the force of the blow will carry through all the boards—or obstacles—in the way.

"Of course, you need to teach people to use the products and recommend them passionately to others, and they need to know the high points of the compensation plan, and above all, to have a deep, abiding respect and pride in Network Marketing itself . . . all that's important. But more than anything else, they must be taught to teach others to succeed."

I stepped out, now dressed, and her voice dropped to normal volume as I appeared.

"That's the selfless quality most every leader in our business possesses. Do you know what I mean when I say 'take a stand' for someone or something?" she asked.

"I think so," I told her. "Taking a stand is like . . . well, 'Stand By Your Man.' How's that for someone who doesn't know anything about country music?"

Rachel laughed, "Very good," she said. "That's what I mean. It's like sticking up for someone—like the Queen's champion in days of old when Knights were bold. In our business, you take a stand for the people you sponsor. You champion them and their success. The shortest and most direct way of doing that is to teach them to teach others.

"Well, truth is," she added, "You teach them to *champion* others, to take a stand for their people. That's what that professor in your story did for his student. He took a stand for what was best in his student. Sometimes, doing that requires your giving people a rough time. Sometimes, being stretched hurts, especially if your mind isn't flexible and isn't used to it.

"That's another benefit of working on your habits of belief. You get used to stretching on purpose. It makes you mentally flexible," she said, and we had reached the front door where her husband was waiting for us.

"So, you want that teacher in the story in *your* Network?" she asked him.

"Sure, wouldn't you?" he asked.

She poked her finger into his chest and said, "I've already got him," kissed him on the cheek with a playful growl, and opening the front door, said, "Let's walk, gentlemen."

CHAPTER FOURTEEN

What's Your Next Step?

The sun had come very close to setting completely as we walked out and down the winding, tree-lined drive way away from the house.

It was a warm evening. The trees' new leaves shimmered as their tops and branches rocked, dancing gently in the welcome breeze. We didn't speak for a long time, the only sound being that of our sneakered footsteps on the blacktop drive.

I was again reflecting on all I had done, and seen, and heard in the last two days. *Two days!* It was weeks' worth—no, more!

I looked over at them, walking hand-in-hand together. They were quite the couple: handsome, beautiful, powerful, success-ful, and yet so real . . . so wonderfully human—all I wanted to be. I suddenly felt an urge to be with my wife Kathy and the kids.

Boy I'd cheated them, I thought. I'd taken myself away, hidden from them as I'd been hiding from everything else. I let out a sigh and looked down at my feet as we were walking.

"He's thinking," Rachel commented.

"He does that," her husband replied.

"Why is he looking down at his feet?" Rachel asked.

"Snakes," her husband said. "He's protecting us from the snakes."

I laughed.

"New habits, my new friend," said Rachel. "The moment you notice you're thinking in old ways, adding to that other side of the scale, just run your movie. Pick a scene—any scene."

"Ahhh . . . " I sighed again, "Is it really that easy?"

"Yes, sir," she said. "It just takes time. Remember how long the old ones took to pile up in there."

"Yeah, I know," I said.

"There's another matter," the Greatest Networker—the male one—added. "And that's, to what are you committed?"

"My wife. My children. Myself. And I'm committed to being a success in this business," I said, looking over at them.

"So, what's your next step?" he asked.

"Gosh," I said, sighing again, and this time allowing *all* the air to leave, leaving me completely empty. As I sucked in my next breath, I leaned my head back and closed my eyes. A flood of images came into the movie theater of my mind.

Scenes of me talking with people, enthusiastically, happily—people with whom I'd been reticent to speak, for some kind of fear or another. People like my boss, at work. Kathy's dad—he was a tough cookie. Others, too . . . strangers, old friends, people I thought wouldn't want to hear what I had to say about Network Marketing. I was talking with all of them now, easily, effortlessly, successfully—and they all loved me for it. Admired me. Respected and trusted me.

I opened my eyes to the growing darkness around me and more pictures flashed across my mind. They just came now. I didn't have to do anything to encourage them.

I thought about making appointments with my wife and kids. Having my children coach me in how to have fun—with them, and with myself, as well. I saw us playing together, rolling down a hill covered with Fall leaves. At Disney World, on rides together, taking pictures with the Disney characters, Mickey Mouse, Goofy . . . I saw us splashing in the surf . . . making things together . . . playing in the snow . . . taking skiing lessons . . . chasing fireflies . . . laughing . . . hugging . . . holding hands . . . reading them stories . . . kissing them goodnight.

There were pictures of my making dates with Kathy for romantic Italian dinners and get-away weekends . . . seeing her in new outfits, bright and beautiful, looking gorgeous, people stopping and staring at her . . . how proud I felt . . . how lucky. She's so wonderful . . . so loving . . . so strong . . . so powerful, too. I saw us in Europe together. I saw the big, deep-bright green emerald ring she's always wanted on her finger. I saw us happier than we've ever been . . . having fun . . . closer . . . talking more together . . . sharing . . . more *in* love.

I saw myself back in Cambridge, laughing with the guys, playing with those new, clunky computers. Being a *real* pioneer. I wanted that—again . . . now, *right now*. I wanted that feeling of doing something few people had ever even dreamed of doing—and having it be a lark . . . a ball . . . a grand and glorious game of discovery and invention.

I saw myself dressed in new suits, Italian, English . . . with real buttonholes . . . made of the most sumptuous, sensual cloth. I looked *fantastic!* Bright ties, matching handkerchiefs . . . elegant . . . with a gold Rolex . . . shaking hands . . . seeing people out of the corner of my eye pointing at me, talking about me . . . how successful I was . . . what a great guy I was . . . how I deserved all my good fortune . . . how they wanted to be like me.

I pictured myself walking in the town of Nara, Japan, down the small, picture-postcard, cobble-stone street in front of Kazuko's precious house. I felt the tranquility of her garden . . . the timelessness . . . the freedom and peace. I felt at home there—on the other side of the world. And I loved having her as my friend. I saw myself all over the world, in China, Russia . . . all kinds of places, talking with friends . . . being welcome . . . valued . . . honored.

I conjured up pictures of me speaking to groups of people about Network Marketing: sitting, speaking earnestly with them. Answering all their questions. I saw myself teaching people . . . reaching out to them . . . caring about them, for them . . . revealing their dreams . . . showing them ways to accomplish their goals they never, ever imagined were possible before. I saw myself as an inspiration for people . . . proof that they could do it, too . . .

"Look at me," I saw myself tell them, "if I can do it, if I can succeed, so can you . . .

"Come on . . .

"Just change your beliefs . . .

"Just know that you make it all up, so you might as well make up living your dreams . . .

"*Come on . . . Come with me.*"

I stopped walking and looked around.

I was alone.

I looked back up the long drive, but there was no one in sight.

I smiled . . . and sighed. They knew, I thought.

They knew.

I walked along the shadowed drive flitting between experiencing the special shapes and sounds of the country evening and the parade of pictures that marched through my mind.

I got to the parking area at the end of the driveway, which was awash with flood light. There was a large piece of paper placed beneath the windshield wipers of my car. I walked over, lifted it free and read the handwritten note.

> *You're welcome to spend the night; your bed is ready.*
> *But we thought you might want to go home and be with*
> *your family. There's a hot cup of tea in a travel mug on*
> *the seat of your car. It will help you stay awake and alert.*
> *Come to the hotel next Thursday. I'm the guest speaker.*
> *Call whenever you want.*
> *You're very special to us.*

I looked up at the house. I placed my hands on my thighs and bowed slightly as I'd seen Kazuko do, and said out loud, "Thank you . . . both . . . all—more than I can ever say." Yes, I thought, I do very much want to be with my family.

I got into my car and drove home.

CHAPTER FIFTEEN

The Beginning

I t's been quite the week," I thought as I drove to the hotel that Thursday after work. If someone would have told me beforehand that the events that happened to me were going to happen, I would never have believed them. But then, I was beginning to believe anything was possible.

"What the mind can believe, *you* can achieve."

Who was that, Clement Stone . . . ? Napoleon Hill . . . ? Me . . . ?

One thing was for certain: I was convinced that all you really needed to do was to *begin* to believe—and accomplishment after accomplishment would follow.

By the time I had returned home from the Greatest Networker's late Saturday night, I'd begun to balance every scale in my mind in my favor—*forever*.

The kids were asleep when I got in, but Kathy was up and we stayed awake 'til dawn talking . . . talking about my weekend, about my old beliefs and new beliefs, about what *she* believed and wanted to replace her old habits with . . . We hadn't done anything remotely like that since we were dating.

Even though I was dead tired from lack of sleep, that Sunday was the most fantastic day. We went to a special place Kathy and I knew since we first arrived here. We hiked back up through the woods with the kids running around, then being carried, then running up and back the trail again. There was a pond we'd discovered long ago and we all went swimming—splashing about, throwing the kids up in the air . . . I cannot remember feeling so free . . . so relaxed . . . so at home with myself and my family.

We all went to that Italian restaurant where the Greatest Networker had taken me for dinner that night. The valet remembered me. The maître d' recognized me and said how it was so nice to see me again. Kathy looked at me and raised her eyebrows. I loved it!

Oh, and *this* you won't believe! Remember, I was the guy who hadn't sponsored a soul? Well, guess what? That week—*three new people!* That's right—*three!* And tonight, two of them were coming to the meeting, and each one was *bringing a guest!* No kidding.

Oh, and that's not the best part. One of the people I sponsored—*my boss!* He'd come into my office the day before, just before lunchtime. He said, "Man, I don't know what you're taking, but I want whatever it is *now!*" I laughed and told him, if he'd buy me lunch, I'd give him a year's worth. He signed up with me right then and there.

And it got even better. My boss said he'd been interested in Network Marketing for a number of years, but he'd heard some conflicting opinions about it and had never really un-derstood it before I explained it. He told me he'd been a teacher right out of college, but the money wasn't any good, and what he really wanted to teach people was about how to succeed in life. "Network Marketing sounds perfect," he said to me. "How do I start?"

Amazing.

Everything was *amazing*.

The truth is, my life had changed 180° in just five days.

I pulled my car up to the front entrance of the hotel. Chris, the doorman I had met the week before, came out and opened the car door before I'd turned the engine off.

I said hello to him and asked if he'd be willing to park my car behind that gray pickup truck, and he said he'd be glad to. I asked him if he was really serious about what he said about going to Japan, and he said he was. So I asked if we could have lunch or dinner and talk about that sometime. He said he'd love that, and we shook hands.

I walked into the hotel room, looking for my new people and their guests. There they were, early—*with two more people than I'd expected!* I became so engrossed in talking with them and asking them questions that I didn't notice the man stand-ing beside me—until, at a break in the conversation, I heard a familiar voice say, "Pardon me, I just wanted to say how great you looked."

I reached out my hand, but he brushed it aside and gave me a big hug, then held me away a little and looked at me. "You really look fantastic," he said. "How are you?"

"I'm even better than I look," I said, and there was more

than a hint of sheer glee in my voice.

He nodded his head up and down and then laughed that patented booming laugh of his.

"I'll just bet!" he said, his smile growing even bigger.

"Meet my friends," I insisted, and he did.

I introduced him to them, and I could tell by the expressions on their faces that coming to their first meeting and being introduced to the Greatest Networker in the World was a tad more than they thought they'd signed on for. It was great! I stood back just a little as he welcomed them and began asking them questions. A couple of times he glanced over at me with an appreciative look and a nod as he learned that I had just sponsored them and how excited they were to be here.

It felt so great!

He turned to me and put one hand on my shoulder, "You are one very quick study, my friend."

"I've had a superb teacher," I replied.

"Thank you," he said, with genuine warmth and a squeeze on my shoulder. "Now," he said with a deep breath and a smile, "are you ready to surpass your teacher?"

I looked into his eyes. There was no expression I could read there—I knew there wouldn't be. I closed my eyes and took a deep breath. Images cascaded through my mind—vivid ones of me as a dynamic, capable and powerful leader.

"Yes," I said, opening my eyes and looking back at him.

"Good," he said. "The meeting's starting. Let's sit down."

The meeting was one of the best I'd attended. The energy was high, there was humor and laughter. It flew along from speaker to speaker and I could tell by the faces of my guests that they were finding it interesting and involving, too—and they were pleased they'd come.

At last, they introduced the Greatest Networker, to an immediate standing ovation speckled with cheers and whistles.

He stood in front of the group, acknowledging our applause. After we'd finished clapping and sat down, he remained standing there silently for a long time, just looking at us. He seemed to take in each and every face in the room.

At last, he spoke.

"Tonight, I am going to show you the secret for success.

"Now, if you're listening *very carefully*, you noticed I said I am going to *show* you the secret. I didn't say I would *tell* it to you.

"You've all heard the secret for success many times—and for some of you, hearing it has made a tremendous difference in your lives—but for most of us, just hearing about something isn't enough.

"Many of you have read about the secret for success, as well. And although some of you have gained much from what you've read, the information alone was not enough to make a profound difference in the way you live and work.

"Do you remember, as a child, how you learned to walk . . . or ride a bicycle?

"You were *shown*.

"You watched grown-ups walking. You saw how they did it. Then, someone walked with you, helped you—picked you up when you fell—all the while holding your hands, as sooner or later you boldly stepped out, moved your legs and you *walked*.

"You were free at last!

"Someone put you on a bike and ran along beside you, holding the seat to keep it steady so you wouldn't fall off—and *showed* you how to do it. And one day—perhaps minutes after you were first *shown* how . . . maybe hours or even days—you *rode* that bicycle. It wobbled. You were afraid, but finally you took off down the sidewalk, *riding the bike* all by yourself.

"You were free at last!

"In each instance, although you knew much about how to walk and ride, that knowledge alone wasn't enough. You *knew* all about *how*, but you couldn't do it—yet. Knowing that information wasn't enough. In fact, what you *knew* was actually of little use to you.

"Looking back on it all, you might assume that what you *thought you didn't know* was the secret. That once you got *that* knowledge, once you learned *that* one thing you knew that you didn't know yet, then you walked . . . then you rode your bike.

"But if you think back very carefully, you'll discover that the secret to walking and the secret to riding did not come from what you knew—and it did not come from what you thought you didn't know, either. That special secret lived somewhere in a vast expanse of unexplored knowledge—what I've learned to call *what you don't know that you don't know*.

"Am I confusing you? I hope not. It's really a very simple idea, but it's the most powerful source of creativity and energy for accomplishment any of us can tap into.

"What walking and riding a bicycle are all about is *balance*. Balance is not something you *have*—like a possession. It's not something you *do*—such as moving this way or that—although both are required to some extent to achieve balance.

"Balance is a state of *being*. You either *are* in that state—or you are not. You are either walking—or falling down; riding—or crashing. Balance is the key.

"Once you attain the state of being balanced, you've got the secret. No one will ever take it away from you. It cannot be lost or stolen. It cannot even be forgotten—although you may experience moments when you don't remember that you remember, but they don't last long.

"So, why am I telling you all of this? Some of you are asking yourselves that very question!" And his booming laugh filled the room as he said, "I can see by some faces that you are. Good!

"I'm telling you this about being *shown* . . . about *what you don't know that you don't know* . . . about *balance* . . . because *success*, having success and doing successful things, is exactly like acquiring *balance*. It is a state of being.

"You are either *being* successful—or you are not. There is no in between. It's a passing or failing grade. Black or white— no gray—like being pregnant.

"So, are you successful? Yes or no?

"*Are you?*"

He paused and again seemed to look at every one of us. For my part, I asked myself the question: yes or no, was I successful? I answered immediately—and out loud, "Yes."

He looked directly at me.

"You answered 'Yes'?" he asked, moving from the podium over to the side of the stage closest to me.

"Will you stand up, please?" he requested.

I did.

"You are successful," he said. "That's wonderful! Tell me, when did you realize that?"

"Sunday," I said.

"This *past* Sunday?"

"Yes," I laughed. "Just this past Sunday." And I could hear the chuckles behind me throughout the audience.

"Please, come up on stage and tell us what happened," he asked.

I took a deep breath and looked at him. He smiled and encouraged me to join him on stage. I went up and stood next to him.

He introduced me to the audience, asked for a microphone for me, and as the man with the mike wired me for sound, he explained how we met.

He told the people about the man he first saw one short week ago, sitting in his hiding place in the back of the room. He reported in specific detail how I had described my business to him, how I had felt about that then, and what I was planning to do—that just this past Thursday I'd been at my "last meeting": I was quitting the business.

He told them about the success I had achieved—sponsoring new people, having my guests present tonight. He described my guests, how they seemed to him excited and enthusiastic about being here . . . how when he spoke with them, they had told him that discovering Network Marketing, finding a place and people who honored their values, that gave them a way to fulfill their life's purpose, was something for which they'd each been searching for years.

He told the audience about my life's purpose as I had shared it with him, the things I valued and what they meant to me, and what they provided for me.

As he spoke, I was touched by the pride that was evident in the way he talked about me. Literally, tears welled up in my eyes and I found myself raising my glasses to wipe my eyes clear, as well. No one had ever said these things about me before. And certainly, no one had ever done so in front of a few hundred people.

He said, I was " . . . an inspiration for him."

He said, he was " . . . so proud of me."

He called me " . . . a young Master."

And then he said, "I promised that I would *show* you the secret for success . . . ."

He put one arm around my shoulder, pointed to me with the other hand, and said, "Here it is."

The silence of the room was a roar in my ears, the faces staring up at me a blur. I had the sensation of falling, yet I knew I was standing . . . floating, yet I knew my feet were firmly planted on the carpeted stage.

An image swept into my mind. It was crystal clear, sharp-edged and vividly bright. It was a room filled with people, seen from the stage. I was the one in front looking out at them. They were standing, applauding, cheering. I had given them something that made a difference to them . . . something that moved and touched them . . . something that empowered them . . . inspired them, and they were acknowledging me. They came up to me on stage. They were shaking my hand. Thanking me. Telling me how much what I had said and done had meant to them.

One woman in particular stood out. She had hold of my

hand in both of hers, and she was saying, "Thank you, thank you so much for showing me my life's purpose . . . for showing me how to believe . . . *in myself.*"

I was snapped out of my movie by the Greatest Networker's arm, still around my shoulders, giving a firm squeeze and then letting go. He stood back and looked into my face and eyes, "You *are* very special to us," he said. "Now, *show* them success." And he walked off the stage.

In an instant, the people were on their feet applauding. There were cheers and people were shouting *my* name. I was in shock. I remember spreading my arms slightly and thanking them, smiling and saying, "Thank you, thank you so much."

As I looked over the standing crowd, the room filled with their enthusiastic applause, I saw him at the back of the room beside the door. Our eyes met. He smiled. And above all the cheers and clapping I heard his booming laugh. He raised his hand, waved to me, and walked out the door.

Amazing!

Epilogue

I f I were you, I think I'd want to know how it all turned out for me. It did—turn out, I mean, and as amazing as it seems (at least it seems that way to me), it's all pretty much the way you'd expect.

That Thursday night five years ago was the first of many, now countless, wonderful evenings, where I've been able to show people what it takes for them to be successful.

It is what I do for a living now.

My Network Marketing business prospered from then on. I've gone on to build an international organization. I'm working on my third book—the first two are industry best-sellers. And, although a precise count is nigh-on impossible to calculate, if I haven't already, I'm certainly well on the way to making a good-sized difference in the lives of millions of people. It is a blessing. I am a very lucky man.

I have achieved pretty stunning success in every area of my life. My relationships and partnerships—especially with my family and friends—are the greatest source of pleasure and satisfaction in my life. I am rich—a millionaire, actually a couple of them by now. I have been to Japan, China and Russia—and lots of other places I never even dreamed of.

And Disney World—remember how much I wanted to take my kids there? Well, we go twice a year now, except it's not just with my kids. Kathy and I take a group of about 50 kids who're part of a program my Network organization and I are involved with that helps abused kids in our city. My own kids get to be the hosts and they dearly love that! So do I.

A fairy-tale life—problem free?

No way! The truth is, I've had more than my share of problems. If anything, as my dreams and achievements grew larger and larger, the roadblocks that seemed to come up got bigger and more impressive, too.

But along the way, I happened upon a life lesson that has given me more freedom than almost any other thing I ever learned. It is simply this:

We ARE that problems are bad.

That we *are* that problems are bad isn't just what we think, and it's not just a feeling we have or wisdom to which we adhere as a truth. It is a way of life for human beings. Usually, we are as unconscious of it as fish are of the water in which they swim. Problems are bad—that's the way it is. That's the way we are. We are born . . . we eat . . . we breathe air . . . and we are that problems are bad.

But what if problems were not good or bad? What if they just *were*? And what if, because problems were just things that happened, we could make them into whatever we wanted, whatever served and empowered us at the time? What if every time a "problem" occured, we chose to have it be fun?

At a certain point, when I was tired of problems being bad, I decided to have them all be as Richard Bach described in his wonderful book *Illusions*:

There is no such thing as a problem without a gift for you in its hands. You seek problems because you need their gifts.

The day I started seeing problems as gifts was the day my life became Christmas and my birthday . . . 365 days a year!

In fact, I could fill another entire book with all the marvelous gifts that have come to me since the fateful evening when I first met the Greatest Networker in the World.

Are you wondering if I finally did buy his house?

Yes, I did.

You may remember I had a vision of sitting in his study office speaking with a young woman, much the way he and I sat there so long ago. That's happened many, many times now.

And if you're wondering, do we see each other? Yes, we do. Our families are quite close.

He and Rachel moved to a plantation in Kauai, in the Hawaiian Islands, about two years ago. We spend Christmas with them there every year. Bobby's in school in Germany. Rebecca opted not to go to college. She's teaching riding at a stable in Virginia. Kazuko goes back and forth from Nara to Hawaii. Everyone's well and happy.

Really, it's just as you'd expect them to be.

When I set out to write this book, I hoped I would do a reasonable job in telling this story as it happened. Now, I feel sure I've done that—but I still have a question.

I wonder—are you convinced, beyond all shadow of even the most fleeting doubt, about the awesome power you have to change your habits of belief?

Do you know, fully and completely, what a tremendous impact doing that will have on your life—and on the lives of countless people whose lives *you* touch?

I hope with all my heart and mind that your answer is "Yes"—now, or soon—that you got it, that you understand the phenomenal creative power and freedom you have to live any way *you choose to believe* is possible.

I know you don't have the Greatest Networker to hang out with. That's okay. You've got this book—and what's more, you've got all the other wonderful books, tapes and marvelous men and women who are masters of this secret for success. And truly, they are *everywhere*—and their lives are devoted to giving the secret away. There are mentors lurking everywhere, just waiting to serve *you*. All you have to do is to go on record as being ready—they'll show up *immediately*.

"*When the student is ready* . . . ."

Mine show up—all the time now.

I thank you for reading my book. And now, I'd like to share with you a simple secret for learning that has served me very well since it was first taught to me: Now that you've read it— read it again. And then, read it a third time. I've read the *Coaching Kids* . . . book at least 20 times since I first saw it that Saturday morning at the Greatest Networker's house—and I've gotten something new from it every time.

When you do read the book again, use it as a flashlight.

There are thoughts, feelings and experiences "neatly scattered" throughout its pages, that will shine new light onto myriad little treasures that are hidden within your own thoughts, feelings and experiences—and that, like your yet to be revealed mentors, are waiting for ready discovery.

And then, ask yourself, "What's next for you?"

One more thing. If you come across somebody in our business who seems like . . . well, like they're ready to explore what they don't know that they don't know yet—lend them your copy of our book. The day you do that may just turn out to be the day that changes their lives for the better—forever.

Have fun.

My best to you.

About the Author

About six years ago, busily involved in my new pursuit of building a Network Marketing business, I got a phone call from an old friend. He had just gotten involved in the same company as I had, and he wanted to know if, by any chance, he happened to be in my downline organization?

No, alas, I informed him, he wasn't.

". . . Well, I have a proposition for you. We work together, I'll tell you everything I know about this business, you tell me everything you know about this business, and I promise you it will be worth your while. What do you think?"

I thought it was a good idea. I still do.

It has been, and keeps being, one of the most fruitful partnerships in my life.

He helped me build a Network organization that continues to be a source of immense satisfaction and fulfillment—as well as a six-figure income. We helped each other create the industry journal *Upline*®, which is a joy for both of us. And now, I've helped him write a book—and even before we'd gotten it to press, I noticed that manuscript copies clandestinely shared were making seismic differences in the lives and Networking careers of people I know.

That was one productive phone call.

17 years!—about half my lifespan to date. Not counting my parents and siblings, I've known John Milton Fogg longer than I have anyone else on the planet who is still an active part of my life.

Since that phone call, John has served as my Network Marketing metal detector. He has a radar-like knack for finding out what there is of value "out there"—what is solid, highly conductive material—and filtering it back in an endless stream of insights. He is a prospector for *understanding*, and much of what he fetches back in his pan is pure gold. I've often heard him claim that his gift lies not in being a great teacher, but in being "a great student." I'm losing track of precisely where we get to draw that line.

It's said that it is a far greater gift to teach a man to fish (thereby feeding him for a lifetime) than to simply catch a fish for him (feeding him for one meal). John has got me catching whole schools of fish—and he's tossing me the best ones he's catching, too! I'm more than fed. To keep up, I've got to open a chain of seafood restaurants. (I wonder if I can Network Market fresh seafood?)

Fortunately, I am not the only one lucky enough to be handed fishing poles and nets by John Milton. He has become a mega-catalyst in the Network Marketing world. Through *Upline*®, thousands of others get monthly fishing lessons. John has also been the barely hidden force (otherwise known as "ghost writer") behind a number of industry best-selling books, scores of newsletters, training materials and promotional pieces.

In his "Acknowledgements," John has singled out some of the extraordinary people who were seminal models for the character of the Greatest Networker. What I get to tell you is that there is a good dose of the autobiographical Mr. Fogg in these pages, too. He's the guy with the Bachelor of Fine Arts . . . with the background in natural foods and marketing . . . his love for and appreciation of Japanese culture and baths, country living in style, "Commitment books," revealing and serving others' values, coaching kids' sports, and peacocks— they're all vintage Fogg.

And like his "author" character, John is " . . . well on the way to making a good-sized difference in the lives of millions of people."

I consider myself a very lucky man to be his partner.

John David Mann
Charlottesville, Virginia

Acknowledgments

"Wow... I just don't know what to say... This is SO unexpected...
First, I'd like to thank the Academy..."

I've always thought that if I ever won an Oscar, they'd have
to pull me kicking and screaming from the stage—I would
have so many people to thank, and I'd insist on telling a story
about why I was thanking each one.

So, here goes.

First of all, I want to thank myself.

Now, that's odd, isn't it? But that is the first thank-you that
comes to mind. And during most of my life to date, I haven't
done too well with acknowledging me. So, now I will. John,
you are an inspiration to me. Thank you.

You will find my mother, Eleanor Haberkorn, and Rachel
and Johnny, my children, on almost every page of this book. I
thank them for the contribution they are to me, and there-
fore, to this book. They are me—and the best of me, too.

My thanks to my partners—all of them. In particular, the
man I hired to be my boss, the sooner-or-later-to-be Senator
from the great state of Virginia, Randolph Byrd. We have our
differences, Byrd and I—and I love and respect no one more.

Thanks to Jim Kossert, John Kalench, Russ and Karen

DeVan, Bill and Sandy Elsberg, Tom "Big Al" Schreiter (and the other member of the board of directors, Susan), William Botsford, Marta Kollman, Ed Clemmons, Richard Poe, Corey Augenstein, Doris Wood, Burke Hedges, Steve Price, Dr. Jay Clark and Linda Reese Young, Len Clements, Dr. Phil Madison, Diana Simmans, Jeff Babener, Linda Chae, Mark and Rene Yarnell, Michael Melia, David Stewart, Tinka Smith, Randy Anderson, Og Mandino, Glen Davidson, Robert and Bonnie Butwin, Robert Natiuk . . . and on and on.

I have found partnership and coaching to be essential for success. These men and women are my partners and coaches.

Last—and rather than "not least," these people deserve very special emphasis:

Carol McCall and Mike Smith, the co-founders of the World Institute for Life Planning: friends, teachers and Master coaches. You will find Carol's and Mike's work throughout this book.

Richard Brooke. You'll find him throughout this book as well. Thanks, Richard.

And finally, my deepest appreciation to my two life-long partners: Susan Anderson Fogg and John David Mann. I would rather die than be without either of them. This book was made possible by them and so is dedicated—as is my life—to them and their life's purpose. — J.M.F.

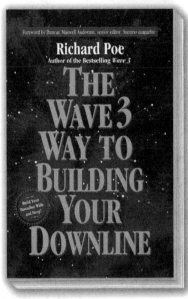

Are You Ready To Make
A Lot More Money In Network Marketing?

If you want to know the secrets to creating walk-away residual income through Network Marketing, you need a subscription to Upline®. In fact, Upline® is the ONLY industry publication that gives you the essential information you need to build a large, exponentially-growing organization. With an Upline® subscription, YOU GET:

- Proven, powerful new business-building **ideas** each and every month
- **Training** from the best in the industry on how to build an organization with money-making staying power
- **Success secrets** of the industry's top money-earners
- Solid, affirmative third-party **validation**
- Money-saving **discounts** of up to 50 percent on the books, tapes and tools you need to reach your goals fast and effectively
- **FREE copyright privileges**—A first class research resource you can reprint and use for training *and* prospecting
- **No** opportunity advertising

Subscribe **NOW** and we'll send you **$30** worth of **FREE** business-building tools with your first issue! Call us **TODAY!**

Get Your Hands ON
The Best Network Marketing Resource
Available—ANYWHERE!

Do you plan to make it big in Network Marketing? If you do, you need tools specific to this industry to grow your business successfully and professionally. Upline® is the only one-stop resource for all your business needs—make one phone call and GET:

- The best, most up-to-date training materials available anywhere in the industry—guaranteed to help you reach your goals in record time!
- The most complete selection of effective, professional prospecting tools
- Software, designed especially for Network Marketers, to help you manage your downline and accelerate its growth
- The best selection of personal and success training for Networkers
- Discounts of up to 50 percent for subscribers of Upline® Journal
- Nearly 300 titles covering the crucial areas of your business—sales leadership, time, money, trends, business development, communication and *much* more!

Take your business to a new level of success—call 800-800-6349 for a FREE Upline® Resources Catalog TODAY or check us out at http://upline.com. See you at the top!